PRAISE FOR *PROFILES IN FREEDOM*

"Carl Higbie has the ability to walk you through history, to open your eyes, and to challenge you to greatness. As a former SEAL team operator, Carl is no stranger to getting to the root of a problem and being real. As you journey through the histories of these American heroes, my sincere hope is that you are encouraged, revitalized, and made more confident. Every history you read is really your own history, no matter when you came to this great country."

From the foreword by US Sen. Markwayne Mullin

"As a Navy SEAL defending freedom, and then an entrepreneur benefiting from our liberties, Carl Higbie provides a unique and essential look at history. A must-read."

Retired Brig. Gen. Blaine D. Holt, US Air Force

"A must-read for every American who wants to learn from our great country's history. I can't wait to share it with my family."

Greg Kelly, anchor of *Greg Kelly Reports* on Newsmax TV, host of *The Greg Kelly Show* on 77 WABC Radio and *The Greg Kelly Podcast*, and author of *Justice for All: How the Left Is Wrong About Law Enforcement*

"Carl Higbie gets it. America was no accident. The greatest nation on Earth was sculpted over centuries by true heroes. Understand how they did it now. Before it's too late."

Sebastian Gorka, PhD, host of *The Gorka Reality Check* on Newsmax TV, and former deputy assistant to President Donald J. Trump

"In an era of revisionist history and agenda-driven education, this book is a breath of fresh air."

Eric Trump, executive trustee and vice president of the Trump Organization

"When people ask what I mean by 'truth, justice, and the American way,' they need look no further than Carl's book about these true American heroes. The amazing men and women profiled here tell the story of America and her founding principles, and why this is the greatest nation on earth."

Dean Cain, American actor, including *Lois & Clark: The New Adventures of Superman*

Profiles in Freedom

Heroes Who Shaped America

Profiles in Freedom

Heroes Who Shaped America

Carl Higbie

Humanix Books

Humanix Books
PROFILES IN FREEDOM BY Carl Higbie
Copyright © 2024 by Humanix Books
All rights reserved

Published by Humanix Books
P.O. Box 20989, West Palm Beach, FL 33416, USA
www.humanixbooks.com | info@humanixbooks.com

Humanix Books is a division of Humanix Publishing, LLC. Its trademark, consisting of the words "Humanix Books," is registered in the United States Patent and Trademark Office and in other countries.

Image credits: chapter openers (US flag art): Andre_BR/Getty Images; page 17: Kean Collection/Getty Images; page 27: Bettmann Archive/Getty Images; page 38: ullstein bild/Getty Images; page 53: Rischgitz/Getty Images; page 68: John Parrot/ Stocktrek Images/Getty Images; page 83: powerofforever/Getty Images; page 94: Alfred Russell/Bettmann Archive/Getty Images; page 110: Bettmann Archive/ Getty Images; page 124: Bettmann Archive/Getty Images; page 138: Paul Popper/ Popperfoto/Getty Images; page 155: Authenticated News/Getty Images; page 170: Andrew J. Russell/ClassicStock/Getty Images; page 186: Keystone View Company/ FPG/Getty Images; page 200: Carol M. Highsmith/Buyenlarge/Getty Images; page 212: Nina Allender/Library of Congress; page 220: George Rinhart/Corbis/Getty Images; page 235: Corbis/Getty Images; page 250: Spooner & Wells/Library of Congress/Getty Images; page 263: The W. Edwards Deming Institute®

ISBN: 9-781-63006-228-6 (Hardcover)
ISBN: 9-781-63006-229-3 (E-book)

Printed in the United States of America

10 9 8 7 6 5 4 3 2 1

DEDICATION

While this book highlights some of the known and unknown heroes in our nation's short history, we will never know all the details about what happened behind the scenes. We will also never know the other people who impacted our heroes in one way or another. Those individuals are forever lost. Their impact remains, but they are forgotten.

That is because impact and influence are often done quietly. Few see it, but the results are very real. If you could somehow trace it back, there would be an evident trail, linking one person to the next and to the next.

This connectedness is real-life influence in action. It's not about fame, importance, or power. It's about impact, lifelong growth, and doing what's right even when others disagree.

So, this book is dedicated to those who challenge others to do good, to be better, and to dream dreams, even if they never get credit for the impact they make.

For me, outside of my family, someone who quietly impacted my life and who never let me slack off is Brad Wallace. You don't know his name, but I do. He added to my foundation so that I could reach higher and go further.

This book is dedicated to him . . . and to you if you are also quietly impacting others around you. Keep it up!

CONTENTS

Foreword

by Markwayne Mullin, US Senator, R-OK

Our history is trying to be rewritten. Schools teach kids to be ashamed of America's past rather than to celebrate it. Now, success is greed, strength is not inclusive, and current generations should apologize for the actions of their ancestors.

The facts, of course, cannot be changed, but that doesn't stop the current trend to retell or simply delete what doesn't fit the current progressive narrative.

Unamerican concepts are being woven into the fabric of our children, trying to indoctrinate our youth to think differently, which always means to think as they do. Their way is the only way.

In many places, it's already happening. New realities and woke agendas are taught to our children in schools, in movies, on TV, on social media, and in the news.

For example, the rise of communism in the 1900s is no longer taught as a bad thing. What bankrupted societies and slaughtered millions upon millions of people is now accepted, promoted, and plastered everywhere as a good thing. The lie only works if people believe it.

Every generation feels it is smarter and more educated than the last, and we really should be, but that is no excuse to forget or cancel those in our past who helped make America into what it is today. Were they perfect? Of course not, but neither are you and neither am I. The woke policies that are popular now will be judged harshly by history. Count on it!

America is great in part because of the struggles we have been through and our drive to always look for answers. We are a nation that thinks independently, that believes in opportunity, and takes action to achieve our dreams. We also live in a country that fosters that reality because of our principles and protection of debate.

History should be taught as it happened and honor those who built the nation that has prospered so greatly. We must teach our children to emulate this success and learn from their blunders. That's what history is for, if we have the guts to be real and learn.

Carl Higbie has the ability to walk you through history, to open your eyes, and to challenge you to greatness. As a former SEAL team operator, Carl is no stranger to getting to the root of a problem and being real.

As you journey through the histories of these American heroes, my sincere hope is that you are encouraged, revitalized, and made more confident. Every history you read is really your own history, no matter when you came to this great country.

We are in this together.

INTRODUCTION

If you were born American in this current sliver of time in the history of mankind, you won the lottery. Think about it. You get to live in a country where you have the freedom to voice your opinion and where economic mobility is entirely in your own hands.

You can get in your car and drive on roads (there was a time when there were no roads at all) from one coast to the other, stopping at any supermarket where the shelves are full of food or stopping at any hotel without worrying about electricity, running water, or food. Nearly everyone you meet along the way has a mobile phone, air conditioning, electricity, and safe drinking water.

We live in a country where one of the primary health concerns is obesity. Think about that! We have it so good, built on the successes of those who went before us, that now we basically have to create things to be angry about.

But our good life was not an accident. It was created on purpose by people with an uncommon drive, and that drive was given to us by our Founding Fathers in the form of a government that offers its citizens the right to achieve as much or as little as they desire.

Built into this amazing form of government is a legislative method to correct possible errors, especially those imposed by law, in the form of many amendments, such as the 13th, 14th and 15th Amendments. Our Founding Fathers wanted to ensure free enterprise in America.

That is the message of America ideals. That is why people brave dangerous deserts, cross shark-infested waters, and hide in storage containers to get here. We are their Promised Land.

But somewhere along the way, we put our guard down. We allowed the progressive Left to selectively pick and choose which parts of America were to be remembered and which were to be canceled. They armed themselves with the tag lines of "anti-racism" and "anti-fascist," claiming to be fighting for people's rights, and we believed them. They used social pressure and public harassment to tear down statues, change educational curriculum, and stop free speech, and we let them.

When I went to school, we said the Pledge of Allegiance every morning, we played dodgeball in gym class, and were taught about our country, and that included the good, the bad, and the ugly. Never in a million years could my parents have imagined a drag queen coming to my elementary school for story time, boys in girls' bathrooms, or Critical Race Theory that stands in the face of Dr. Martin Luther King Jr.'s entire philosophy.

Back in the 70s, there was no problem with a kid having a gun in his car on school grounds in hopes of getting out early enough to catch a quick hunt before heading home. And 50 years before that, in some areas of the country, kids even brought their guns into the classroom . . . and there were no mass shootings.

I remember religion being taught in school, not as indoctrination, but as a history that those were the principles our system of government and way of life were founded upon.

When I graduated public high school in 2002, I had learned how to change a tire, stay in shape, cook a healthy meal, and even how to sew a shirt. Now, high school kids can't even do a load of laundry, not to mention suffering through a dumb fad of eating laundry detergent!

The grossly liberal educational system has swung the pendulum so far from what our nation was founded upon that they are trying to reinvent our history. Strangely, they cry victim and demand inclusion, while stripping away every aspect of history that they don't agree with.

They try to silence voices of reason. They try to remeasure by their liberal progressive standards our historical heroes who made an impact on our country. They must redefine everything to fit their narrative. They don't teach our actual history because they hope that by ignoring it we will forget, for when it's forgotten, it is effectively erased.

But people should not be erased, nor should our history. We should learn from it and grow, always climbing higher than the previous generation. We are supposed to be smarter, faster, and accomplish more than our parents.

Those who cancel others are not leaders. They have nothing to offer of their own. If they did, they would get out in front and make things happen, and their cause would become the cause of the masses because it's worth fighting for.

To simply cancel others, especially our nation's history and the people who made this nation great, is cowardice. It is small-minded thinking. And it is futile. After all, to forget history is to repeat it. The problem is that it takes an awful long time to get back to a point of strength.

But Ronald Reagan did warn us in his 1989 farewell address:

"If we forget what we did, we won't know who we are. I'm warning of an eradication of the American memory that could result, ultimately, in an erosion of the American spirit."

Those who helped build this country lived and died for their ideals so that we could have a better life. The wise will not only build on that, but they will teach their children to do the same.

CHAPTER 1

Thomas Dermer

1590-1620

If you have never heard of Thomas Dermer, don't feel bad. Very few people know the name. What's more, he lived for only 30 years, so he had to make it count.

Lucky for us, he did.

When Dermer sailed our shores, we were not yet the United States. We weren't even 13 Colonies. Dermer was busy exploring the coastline before the Pilgrims arrived in 1620 and established the Plymouth Colony in what would eventually become Plymouth, Massachusetts.

Born in 1590 back in Plymouth, England, Dermer sailed first to our shores in 1614 with the now well-known Captain John Smith. Up and down the coast Dermer would sail, and back and forth to England.

His job as navigator and explorer was mostly a pioneering venture, going where no one had gone before and bringing some sense of order so that others could follow. That meant taking risks that few, even in his day and age, would consider.

In addition to working with John Smith, Dermer also worked with several companies that not only traded but also helped establish settlements in the New World. The British Newfoundland Company (established in 1610) was one such company. They first brought settlers to the southeastern island of Newfoundland, which is now part of Canada.

He also worked with the Plymouth Company, another British company chartered by none other than King James himself (in 1606) that was trying to bring settlers to the east coast of what would eventually be Massachusetts. This would be the Pilgrims on the *Mayflower* arriving in the latter part of 1620, but by the time they stepped ashore, Dermer would be dead.

Establishing some sort of dialogue with the Native American Indians was of course necessary before there could be successful trade and safe settlements. This task fell upon Dermer. Maybe he volunteered for it, as it was his nature as a pioneer, or maybe it was his job, but either way, he was very good at it.

Perfect Timing

It was in Newfoundland that something amazing happened. It was the coming together of the right people who just so happened to meet up at precisely the right time. Some call it fate or providence or the stars aligning, but I see it as God orchestrating things to our benefit. Whatever you call it, it was fortunate.

There in Newfoundland, Dermer met a Patuxet Indian by the name of Tisquantum, who we have grown up calling Squanto.

At the same time, a plague had been ravaging the different Indian tribes along the coast of what would eventually be the states of Massachusetts and Maine.

This plague ran for several years (estimated to be 1616–1619) and nearly killed everyone it touched. The empty villages littered with bones from people who died and were never buried would not be reinhabited by other Indians because none of them knew the cause or if the same fate awaited them.

This left a wide portion of the coastal land open and empty, just waiting for British settlers.

66 He who does not work, will not eat. 99

– CAPTAIN JOHN SMITH

We don't know exactly what the plague was, but it didn't affect the settlers as much as it did the locals, and it was here before the Pilgrims arrived. Some reason the plague came from a French ship that came ashore in the area. Most of the sailors were killed, but a few were taken captive by the Indians. A "European" plague could have easily spread from there, killing those (the local Indians) who had never been exposed to the virus that had probably plagued Europeans for years.

Interestingly, Dermer would end up rescuing a couple of these same French sailors who had been kidnapped. What are the odds of that?

It turns out that Squanto, along with more than 20 other Indians, had been deceived and kidnapped several years earlier and sold as slaves in Spain. Amazingly, some Spanish friars stepped in at some point and redeemed them. Maybe they bought them or maybe they applied pressure to the right people, I don't know, but they saved the day.

Eventually, Squanto ended up in England where he met and mastered English with the help of John Slany, who was treasurer for the very Newfoundland Company that employed Dermer.

While Squanto was in Europe, the Patuxet were wiped out by the mysterious plague. He didn't know it yet, but he was literally the last person alive from his entire tribe.

When Squanto and Dermer met up in Newfoundland, the final piece of the puzzle fell into place. Dermer had the perfect interpreter who not only knew the local languages but also knew the area, and that meant he could get much more done much more quickly.

No doubt after some serious discussions and a lot of trust on Squanto's part, they sailed back to England in 1618 and met with the leaders of the Plymouth Company. The Plymouth Company was planning to settle in New England and needed help with preparation on the ground. Dermer and Squanto were exactly what the company needed.

The deserted shores of Massachusetts would end up being where the Plymouth Company established their settlement, despite all their New England planning, but they didn't know it at the time.

Dermer was given command of an expedition to New England. He and Squanto were tasked with scouting out the land for the company, meeting with local Indian tribes, and doing anything and everything possible to prepare for the 1620 arrival of the settlers.

Diplomacy

Together, Dermer and Squanto accomplished what had never been done before. They helped, for the first time, bring Native American Indians and Europeans together to talk, discuss, and plan.

Obviously, other Indians had been to Europe, including the legendary Pocahontas, but this marked the beginning of real conversations, actual diplomacy, between Indians and Europeans.

The Pilgrims wanted peaceful relations with the Indians before they even arrived, so they paid special attention to everything Dermer wrote in his many letters to the Plymouth Company. They didn't know it at the time, but Dermer and Squanto would be part of the reason they would survive their journey to the New World!

Dermer's ship arrived at what would eventually be Maine in 1619. He and Squanto, along with some of the crew, sailed farther south toward Squanto's homeland and his Patuxet tribe. When they arrived, his village was deserted. The surrounding villages were also empty.

> 66 All great and honorable actions are accompanied with great difficulties, and both must be enterprised and overcome with answerable courage. 99
>
> – WILLIAM BRADFORD, GOVERNOR OF THE PLYMOUTH COLONY, WHO ARRIVED ON THE *MAYFLOWER* IN 1620

The plague had killed virtually everyone for miles and miles around.

If I were Squanto, I would have had a terrible mix of emotions—anger, resentment, fear, appreciation, and loss. His family was dead. Maybe he had brothers and sisters. Maybe he had a girlfriend or fiancée. But everyone was dead.

I can't even imagine that.

They ventured farther inland, looking for survivors, perhaps evaluating the land for the Plymouth Company, when they finally came to a village that wasn't uninhabited.

The Indians were not so friendly and would have killed Dermer had it not been for Squanto. Apparently, and rightfully so, the Indians were still angry with the Europeans (British and Spanish alike) who had kidnapped and enslaved their people.

Perhaps Squanto told them of his own enslavement and eventual return. Maybe some of those who were kidnapped with Squanto had come from this same village and Squanto was able to tell what had happened to them. Whatever the case, Squanto deserves credit for interceding and saving Dermer's life.

It was here with these Indians that Dermer was able to free two French sailors who had been captive for several years.

They all returned to the ship anchored at Squanto's very-empty Patuxet village and continued exploring.

For the next year, Dermer (sometimes with Squanto, sometimes without) sailed meticulously into every harbor looking for good land and perhaps gold and trade opportunities for the company.

He spent the winter of 1619 in Jamestown, Virginia, the first successful settlement by settlers from England. The next spring, he headed north to New England to continue his work for the Plymouth Company.

" More than 30 million people can trace their ancestry to the 102 passengers and approximately 30 crew aboard the *Mayflower* when it landed in Plymouth Bay, Massachusetts, in the harsh winter of 1620. "

– ACCORDING TO MAYFLOWER400UK.ORG

Somewhere along the way, he wrote in a letter that he planned to stop again at Squanto's deserted Patuxet village. Captain John Smith had marked this spot, Squanto's village, on a map as Plymouth. In the letter, Dermer recommend that spot as a likely place for a settlement.

It turns out that the *Mayflower* and her crew, because of rough seas, wind, and shoals that proved too difficult to sail through, would end up at this very location late that year. It would be the Pilgrims' landing, the second English settlement, and the start of the Plymouth Colony.

Just south of this location, Dermer landed at a place where he had previously traded with the Indians. Unexpectedly, the Indians attacked, severely wounding Dermer.

He was able to get into the landing party's small boat and, with the help of one sailor left alive, make it back to his ship. They sailed hastily back to Virginia, but it was too late. Either the wounds, the infection, or both were too much, for Captain Thomas Dermer would die there in Jamestown.

The ideal man for the job, the first diplomat between Europeans and Native American Indians, was gone.

I wonder what else he could have accomplished if he had lived another 30 years! We will never know. But if I could somehow ask Dermer a few questions, I would ask him:

First, can you tell me more about your diplomacy efforts between the settlers and the Indians? Why treat people as equals when others did not?

Second, what advice would you give to both settlers and Indians that might help as the nation expands farther and farther west?

Third, could you buy or claim some land for me on one of the islands you scouted? Having a chunk of Martha's Vineyard would be worth a pretty penny today!

We all would sit spellbound for hours if we could hear Dermer speak about his travels, the beauty of the raw and untouched land, and his experiences with the Indians.

As for Squanto, he went on to be an invaluable resource to the Pilgrims, especially in the first year as the settlers had so much to learn. He rightfully earned his place in American history.

Two years after Dermer, Squanto would die as well. In his case, it was Indian fever, which he caught while guiding Governor William Bradford around Massachusetts.

You could say Thomas Dermer (and Squanto as well) was one of the many pillars that make up the initial foundation of this country. He literally gave his life so that we could have a better one.

He was just one of many heroes who have done that for our country, and I salute him.

Thomas Dermer William Bradford
1590–1620   1590–1657

Thomas Dermer worked for the Plymouth Company that established the Plymouth Colony, of which William Bradford would be governor. They may have met in the years prior in England while planning for the 1620 voyage. Bradford later read Dermer's letters and settled in Plymouth, Massachusetts, as Dermer recommended.

CHAPTER 2

William Bradford

1590-1657

an you imagine being tossed back and forth in cramped quarters on a ship for more than two months? Then trying to live through a freezing cold Massachusetts winter with very little food, with sickness that brought death, all while trying to keep adults and children alive?

Me neither.

But that was the welcome that the Pilgrims of 1620 received when they landed in the New World! More like a very old, primitive world, but about half of them miraculously survived.

In fact, more than 30 million Americans today can trace their family tree back to this group of pioneers. Doing the math, that's almost 1 in 10 Americans who owe some thanks and gratitude to those in their family history who fought through the harsh conditions and kept going despite the odds.

I love that about our American history. They were fighters, not quitters. They were builders, creators, inventors, and dreamers. That is what our nation is made from, and that is what will always lift its people up.

Of this ragtag group, there were many leaders who would stand up and make their mark on history. One of them was William Bradford.

The Unlikely Beginnings of William Bradford

Orphaned at age seven, raised by his grandparents, and too sickly to play or work outside, Bradford didn't have much going for him. He filled his alone time with reading, and much of that was the Bible, which may have been the best way to prepare for the future during that time.

> 66 Every child in America should be acquainted with his own country. He should read books that furnish him with ideas that will be useful to him in life and practice. As soon as he opens his lips, he should rehearse the history of his own country. 99
>
> – Noah Webster

Born in 1590 in England, he was a teen when the Separatist movement (which were simply Christians wanting to create their own local churches rather than be controlled by the Church of England) began to make waves. They just so happened to meet in a nearby town, and Bradford joined them.

By the mid-1600s, being a Separatist was fine, but not when it first began. Persecution in every form was the reality of staying in England, so the Separatists, led by William Brewster and John Robinson, pulled up their roots, and together they all moved to Holland. It was 1608, and young Bradford went with them.

Holland would not be their permanent home. They longed for a place where they could be free to live as they chose it, rather than be told what to do by church, country, or customs.

During the 12 years that they were there, Bradford grew up, got married, and had a son.

While there, they heard of a New World where they could actually be free. Since England claimed ownership of this New World, the Separatists had to request permission to go. They received it and began to make plans for their 1620 departure.

Much of the paperwork, record keeping, and correspondence between government officials and those financing the trip, not to mention other details with the planning of the voyage, fell to Bradford. He had a knack for it, and it no doubt helped later when he was elected governor.

Their intended destination—which they would never reach—was the northern corner of the land allotted to the Virginia Colony.

Bradford was 30 years old when he and his wife, Dorothy, set sail. They left their son in the Netherlands with Dorothy's parents. The boy was only a few years old, and they feared for his safety. It was a smart move, for many children died that winter. Years later, their son would also make the voyage.

66 Just as one small candle may light a thousand, so the light here kindled hath shone unto many. 99

– WILLIAM BRADFORD

The plan was to take two ships from England, but one of them wouldn't stop leaking, so everyone and everything was put onto one ship, the *Mayflower*.

Other non-Separatists were allowed to join them in the venture to help cover the required costs. These were people more interested in economic freedom than religious freedom, but together they would form the second settlement by the British. Jamestown in Virginia was the first.

They sailed for the New World in September of 1620.

Off to the New World

It is here that I would like to ask some questions. Maybe Bradford had answers. If I could, I would ask him:

1. First, why are you sailing into winter? You aren't going to the Caribbean, so you know it's not going to be a hot, sunny Mexican cruise.

2. Second, do you think you can plant crops in winter? Ships have a limited amount of food supplies, so planting and growing crops is immediately necessary. Arriving in winter means eating the stored supplies and not planting until spring.

3. Third, why so many children? There are 35 kids and 102 adults. That's more than a third as children, who cannot work much and yet need to be fed, clothed, and protected. I understand wanting to keep a family together, but they could always come over later.

Maybe someone misled them, maybe they were under such pressure that it didn't matter when they left, I don't know, but they really could not have chosen a more terrible and dangerous time to sail into the unknown.

Everyone who made it through the first winter was lucky to be alive. Sadly, more than half of them died, including men, women, and children.

Bradford himself got sick but recovered. Dorothy was one of the unluckiest ones of all. She never made it to shore. She fell overboard and drowned as it was anchored just off the coast of the New World. Some of the men, including, Bradford, were ashore exploring at the time. She was buried on land.

The governor of their settlement, John Carver, didn't last long either. He died that winter. Bradford was elected governor in his place and would be re-elected governor over and over for the next 35 years.

There was something else that Bradford did well, besides that of being governor, and that was writing. He wrote, journaled, and took notes about his life and the lives of the settlers in the New World. Much of what we know today about the Plymouth Colony and the first Thanksgiving of 1621 and the Native American Indians who helped them, came from his written record.

Landing in the upper part of the Virginia Colony (near present-day New York) was their intended destination, but the weather was so bad that they had to choose an alternate location.

In the end, they chose a bay and a spot within that bay that Captain John Smith had marked on a map as Plymouth. It would become Plymouth, and eventually Plymouth, Massachusetts.

Bradford later wrote about the location:

"Captain Thomas Dermer had been here the same year that the people of the *Mayflower* arrived, as appears in an account written by him, and given to me by a friend, bearing date, June 30th, 1620."

Thomas Dermer, who worked for the Plymouth Company and was killed just a few months before the *Mayflower* arrived, had recommended that very spot as a good location. It was the previous site of Squanto's home village of his Patuxet tribe, which was still deserted after the plague had come through a few years earlier.

> 66 If you read in front of your kids, it's very likely that they'll become readers too. 99

— JOHN LITHGOW, DESCENDENT OF WILLIAM BRADFORD

The famous interpreter and Native American Indian, Squanto, would soon play an important role in helping Bradford and the entire Plymouth Colony.

A few days before Christmas, everyone went ashore and began constructing houses as quickly as they could. The settlers had arrived, and so began their race for survival.

Bradford the Leader

Thanks to Bradford's leadership skills, he was able to keep the settlers together and focused on efforts that would help everyone survive. When the *Mayflower* sailed back to England, none of the settlers left. Only the crew returned. That was their job as hired crew. Unfortunately, half of the crew had died as well during the horrible winter.

To me, that not only shows how committed they were to each other and the overall vision, but it shows how well Bradford kept the team together. If there had been hypocrisy, infighting, and discontent among them, people would have left. Instead, they all stuck around, and that shows Bradford was a top-notch leader.

Bradford was also intent on working with and creating good relations with the local Native Americans. Squanto was only one of the local Indians who helped the settlers survive.

Massasoit, chief of an Indian tribe nearby that somehow missed the death plague that had wiped out Indians for hundreds of square miles, helped the settlers with their food supply.

But it was Squanto who was especially practical. This was, after all, his home turf. He knew the area as this was where his tribe used to live. He taught the settlers how to fertilize their fields of corn, where to fish, how to catch eels, and other secrets that significantly improved their lives.

William Bradford later described Squanto as "a special instrument sent of God for their good beyond their expectation."

That is why the settlers who made it through the first winter were so thankful as they headed into their second winter. They had better homes and food stored away. They had made it, and there was hope!

The first Thanksgiving celebration, shared between the settlers and Indians, would be the start of our national holiday. Oddly, it wouldn't become an official holiday until 1863 when Abraham Lincoln declared it so.

Squanto served as interpreter and guide, as he had with Thomas Dermer and John Smith. Sadly, while guiding Bradford and his men (near present day Chatham, Massachusetts, just inland off Cape Cod), Squanto fell sick and died a few days later.

It was "Indian fever," according to Bradford, and "his death was a great loss."

Each year, the Plymouth Colony grew. Other ships came, packed with settlers and Separatists alike, marriages were performed, children were born, and the town expanded. Even Bradford remarried, to Alice Southworth in 1623, a widow with two sons. She was a Separatist, one of the many who had stayed in Holland when the others left for the New World.

" The 'wall of separation between church and state' is a metaphor based on bad history, a metaphor which has proved useless as a guide to judging. It should be frankly and explicitly abandoned."

– WILLIAM REHNQUIST, DESCENDENT OF WILLIAM BRADFORD

Bradford's young son, who had stayed behind in Holland, joined him. Also, he and Alice had three more children together. All six of their children would reach adulthood, get married, and have children of their own.

Interestingly, being related to William Bradford is a lineage that people are proud to have. Not that they can do anything about it, but the fact that it's seen as a good thing is intriguing.

A few notable descendants[1] of Bradford's include:

- Noah Webster, creator of the Webster's Dictionary
- Actors: Christopher Reeve, Clint Eastwood, John Lithgow, Sally Field, and the Baldwin brothers
- Frank Nelson Doubleday, publisher
- Julia Child, chef
- George Eastman, founder of Eastman Kodak Company
- William Rehnquist, Chief Justice on the Supreme Court

In time, the community grew and expanded, eventually becoming the Massachusetts Bay Colony. About the time the

[1] https://familypedia.fandom.com/wiki/William_Bradford_(1590-1657)/List_of_Famous_Descendants

colony was a teenager, people began to move farther inland. It was a sign of the strength of the colony for groups of people to launch out on their own, which meant Bradford had done a good job.

After 10 years of hard, grueling work, perhaps Bradford had more free time, for it was then that he began to write about the Plymouth Colony. He described the initial *Mayflower* voyage, the first winter, the Indians who helped them, life in the colony, and even listed the settlers and their families.

He kept writing for many years, giving us an incredible picture of early life in America. He also continued to govern, up until a few months before his death. He died after an illness in 1657.

His wife, Alice, would live for another 13 years, dying in 1670. Both are buried in Plymouth, Massachusetts.

> 66 A good reputation is measured by how much you can improve the lives of others. 99
>
> – GEORGE EASTMAN, DESCENDENT OF WILLIAM BRADFORD

Looking back, Bradford was the perfect leader for their situation. He successfully juggled so many pieces, such as the religious freedom for the Separatists, the economic needs of the whole settlement, the financial elements of the colony and the ships, the relationships with local Indians, the practicals of farming, fishing, hunting, and the tracking of every important detail that kept it all together.

He must also have been as strong as an ox, having survived the rough seas, loss of a wife, brutal cold, extreme conditions, trekking through untamed wilderness, boating through dangerous waters, encountering Native American Indians, and sickness that killed more than half of the first settlers. He had come a long way from his days as a sickly young boy.

If you are one of the fortunate Americans who can trace your lineage back to the settlers who landed in Plymouth that winter in 1620, or even to the direct lineage of William Bradford, you know you are lucky to be here.

We all benefited by the life of William Bradford and his efforts with the Plymouth Colony.

So next time you are sitting down at Thanksgiving, enjoying your family and food, be thankful for all you have. Others paid the price so you can enjoy your life today, William Bradford among them.

William Bradford		**William Penn**
1590–1657		1644–1718

William Penn may have read William Bradford's first-hand account of the Pilgrims and their survival in the New World and the first Thanksgiving while in bed as a sickly teen. *Mourt's Relation*, the booklet that told the first year of the Pilgrim's adventures in Plymouth, was published in London in 1622. Also, both Penn and Bradford knew first-hand the persecution by the church and Crown.

CHAPTER 3

William Penn

1644-1718

Imagine being given more than 25,000,000 acres! Yes, as in *25 million* acres! That's too much to wrap my brain around, especially in today's reality where a house is typically bought on a quarter acre or less.

But this was back in the day when England (in addition to the French, Spanish, Dutch, Swedish, and others) laid claim to large portions of the country and could give out land the size of an entire state. And that's exactly what happened, even if I still can't quite imagine it.

Apparently, an admiral in the British Navy had loaned the King of England a lot of money (about $700,000 in today's value) during a desperate time. He also helped capture the island of Jamaica from Spain in 1655, which in itself was a prize and profit center for the Crown.

The admiral was definitely owed something big for all he had done, but he would die in 1670, his loan never repaid.

Then, in 1681, the admiral's son, William Penn, made a proposal to the king. Would he, King Charles II, grant land in the New World as a way to settle the old debt? Situated below New York, above Maryland, and west of the Delaware River, the requested land was land that the Crown claimed to own.

The king agreed! And suddenly, William Penn had his own state, even though it wouldn't become a US state until 1787. Also, the actual boundaries would prove contentious for years to come, but at the time it didn't matter.

"I think I'll name it Sylvania," Penn is reported to have said.

"That's lame," the king probably replied. "Call it Pennsylvania, after your father."

And so it was. The Pennsylvania colony or Commonwealth of Pennsylvania, and eventually just Pennsylvania, was born.

What to Do with Your Own State

William Penn had big plans for his 40,000 square miles, and he immediately went to work. A square mile contains 640 acres, and many places in the US were measured that way, with fields, roads, and city streets laid out accordingly.

Go online and check it out. An aerial view of mid-western farmland or cities will often reveal such a layout. I'd settle for just one square mile, let alone 40,000 of them!

Penn made offers that few could refuse, including selling his land in as small as 100-acre sections for just 40 British shillings. Now, 20 shillings equals 1 British pound (£1), so that meant he was selling 100 acres for a mere 2 pounds (£2).

That's ridiculously cheap! Based on how much £2 was worth back then in comparison to today's dollar value, that would be somewhere around $400–$500 for 100 acres or $4–$5 per acre.

Would you not agree that those were more than generous terms? Imagine that! If only you and I could buy land at that price today. Simply incredible! I'd buy every acre I could afford and borrow money from every friend and family member I knew. And that's probably what some of the original purchasers did.

Penn was not only smart, but he was also good at marketing. He advertised his land offerings in different languages throughout Europe, and people from all over England and other parts of Europe took him up on the opportunity. Ship after ship sailed to the New World and their new home of Pennsylvania.

> William Penn's home sits on the bank of the Delaware River. Built around 1682, it holds the distinction of being the country's first brick house.

By 1700, the greatest real estate agent of perhaps all time had sold more than 800,000 acres.

Penn had a plan and purpose for all he was doing. It wasn't a secret plan by any means. In fact, his plan might have helped the king approve of his massive land grant.

You see, William Penn was a Quaker, and Quakers faced intense persecution in England, as did many other Christian sects or denominations, and that naturally made them want to leave for a safer, more prosperous life in another country.

That was part of the plan and purpose for Pennsylvania.

The Quakers were also a bit of a bother to the king and the established church. Getting them out of the country would be a good thing. Maybe that wasn't the only reason the king approved of Penn's request, but I'm guessing that getting thousands of these "troublemakers" out of London, out of politics, and out of the local prisons was probably seen as a smart move.

> 66 If thou wouldst rule well, thou must rule for God, and to do that, thou must be ruled by him . . . Those who will not be governed by God will be ruled by tyrants. 99
>
> – WILLIAM PENN

What made the Quakers so contentious was their pacifism (they opposed war), their refusal to swear allegiance to anyone, and their belief that you could follow God and hear from Him without a priest. They also dressed very plainly, treated everyone as equals, and used "thee" and "thou" when they talked. I'm sure most people could put up with their clothes, mutual respect, and speech, but not fighting for your country, now that would have made any king angry.

This last part of the Quaker beliefs really upset Penn's father, admiral that he was of the British Navy, and he came close to disowning his own son. However, before he died in 1670, he and young Penn were able to reconcile their relationship.

Building Pennsylvania

When I was a kid, I always thought the smiling Quaker on boxes of Quaker Oats was William Penn, but apparently (so says the Quaker Oats Company) that it is not the case.

What I also did not know (somehow, I missed that in history class) was just how much of a role Penn played in the state of Pennsylvania and in our country as a whole.

In Pennsylvania, Penn wanted to create a place where everyone had equal rights, especially in the areas of:

- freedom of religion (he had been excommunicated, expelled, fined, beaten, and jailed for being a Quaker).
- fair trials (he had fought for that already and had been imprisoned without a trial).
- free elections (no community can survive without that).
- elected representatives (rather than powerful people appointing their puppets).
- separation of powers (different groups held power, yet together they ruled for everyone's benefit).

Of course, Penn didn't know it at the time, but his democratic template for Pennsylvania not only attracted a lot of people, it also laid the groundwork for the eventual success of the state of Pennsylvania, and the state in turn laid the groundwork for the success of the nation.

Penn was much more than just a lawyer. He was an entrepreneur, visionary, peacemaker, author, leader, public servant, and family man. Above all, to me, he was a long-term thinker.

I think he knew what religious and financial freedom-seeking people really wanted, because he had been at the short end of that stick many times, and because he was a clear thinker and good communicator, he was able to convey his message well.

Our nation always needs people like him. Now we need them desperately!

Unfortunately for Penn, he had so many pressing issues back in England that he was only able to spend a total of four years (two two-year stints) in Pennsylvania. But being in another country didn't stop him from helping build Pennsylvania.

Here are just a few examples of his long-term thinking that made a positive impact in Pennsylvania and the eventual future of the United States of America:

1. He purposefully tried to foster a good relationship with the Native American Indians, paid them what was considered to be a fair price for their land, and even took the time to learn their language so he could communicate directly with the Indians.

2. He established laws in Pennsylvania that made sure everyone had a fair trial—Indians included—with a jury of their peers. That little detail many years later made it directly into our Bill of Rights!

3. He and his team carefully planned out the city of Philadelphia, which not only became a thriving city, but it was also intentionally full of green space for farming or parks. He had witnessed the Great Fire of London in 1666 that burned thousands of buildings, and he did not want that to happen to his city.

4. He did have absolute authority in Pennsylvania, second only to the king, but he created a democratic system that could function without him. His democratic system would be copied by many other states and would be part of the US Constitution!

5. He started the William Penn Charter School (K–12) in 1689 in Philadelphia, and it's still in use today. As for William Penn University, it was named in his honor, but founded in 1873.

Believe it or not, Penn and his family had a hard time making their Pennsylvania charter turn a profit. His three sons who inherited the land may have had the title of chief proprietor or governor, but they also had their own trades back in England from which they supported themselves.

Some of his financial troubles, however, were the result of people trying to rip him off. His own financial advisor cheated him out of much of his profits from Pennsylvania land sales and later tried to steal the whole of Pennsylvania from him. Penn spent years in English courts arguing his case.

He also had to contend directly with the fickleness of the Crown. He fell out of their good graces, based on political happenings or dominant voices at the time, and then fell back into their good graces the next. The Crown itself changed hands repeatedly. King Charles II, who gave him Pennsylvania, died in 1685. His brother, King James II, was deposed in 1688. And on it went. And each change undermined Penn and his efforts in Pennsylvania.

Imagine this sequence of events for Penn:

- charged with treason
- thrown in jail
- branded a traitor
- estates in Ireland are taken by the Crown
- Pennsylvania is taken away
- exonerated
- Pennsylvania is returned
- most of his estates in Ireland are returned

What a wasted effort! But he could never get back his time, or the money lost defending himself. Or reverse the unhealthy effects of being locked up in a British prison, or the bad name that was so freely thrown about by powers that be.

In 1712, it is said that he suffered a stroke that was so debilitating to his mind, body, and speech that he required constant care from his wife for the last six years of his life.

Penn died in 1718 and was buried in an unassuming Quaker graveyard in Jordans, England, just outside of London.

Hannah Penn – First Woman Governor

As if the infighting over Pennsylvania was not enough, it only continued after Penn's death. In fact, the wrestling of control over Pennsylvania would continue for the Penn family until after the American Revolution! Even Benjamin Franklin would get involved.

Penn was first married in 1672 to Gulielma Springett. She bore several children, including William Penn Jr. She was ill for many years and died in 1694. She rests in the same graveyard as Penn.

> 66 Let men be good, and the government cannot be bad. If it be ill, they will cure it. But if men be bad, let the government be ever so good, they will endeavor to warp and spoil it to their turn. 99
>
> – WILLIAM PENN

Two years later, Penn married Hannah Callowhill, who was more than 25 years younger than him. Three of their sons would play a role in the management of Pennsylvania.

When Penn died, his will stated that Pennsylvania was to go to Hannah and their children. William Penn Jr. was given much of the estates that Penn had in Ireland, but not Pennsylvania. Penn Jr. contested this in British court, but Hannah and her family, as the will directed, were able to win their case.

Hannah knew how to handle herself in court. She had successfully refuted Lord Baltimore of Maryland and his claim to east Pennsylvania and the entire city of Philadelphia during the years that Penn was a virtual invalid. She also proved herself to be a very capable governor.

Being the first woman governor would have required an extra level of guts, steel, brains, and nerve. Thankfully, Hannah had all of that, with plenty to spare.

Hannah managed everything about Pennsylvania during the six years that Penn was ill. She ruled in his place. When he died, it was only natural that she continue in her role as governor. She did so for eight years until she died in 1726. She would be buried beside William.

Interestingly, in 1984, by an act of Congress, William and Hannah Penn were given honorary US citizenship. She was the first woman in US history to receive this honor.

After Hannah's death, her sons managed and maintained ownership of Pennsylvania up until 1775 when the last son died. Pennsylvania would soon change hands once more.

The government of Pennsylvania (after the American Revolution, which started in 1775 and ended in 1783) dissolved the Penn proprietorship and paid the Penn family £130,000 (British pounds) for back-rent and the entire 25,000,000 acres. That was quite a deal!

It may have been the end of the Penn family owning Pennsylvania, but it was only the beginning of Pennsylvania as a US state.

Years Later in Penn's Philadelphia

Penn's Philadelphia is situated right on the Delaware River in the far eastern side of the state. Its position, halfway between New York and Washington, D.C., was perfect for what was to come.

Philadelphia would go on to play a special role in American history, including:

- **The first public library:** In 1731, Benjamin Franklin and several others formed a group, raised money, and ordered books from England as part of their effort to create a public library. They asked James Logan, who had been William Penn's secretary, to select the first batch of books for the library.
- **Founding Fathers:** Philadelphia would be the hub, the go-to place, where the nation's Founding Fathers would get together and think, plan, strategize, and write.
- **Liberty Bell:** Housed in Philadelphia's Independence Hall, the Liberty bell is inscribed with these words: "Proclaim Liberty Throughout All the Land Unto All the Inhabitants Thereof." Installed in 1751, it is thought that the words (a verse from the Bible) honor William Penn who brought freedom of religion and democracy to Pennsylvania.

- **Continental Congress:** The First and Second Continental Congress meetings took place in Philadelphia in 1774 and 1775, with the likes of George Washington, John Adams, Patrick Henry, Samuel Adams, Benjamin Franklin, and scores of others in attendance.
- **Declaration of Independence:** Probably the most important document in all American history, the Declaration of Independence was written and signed in Philadelphia.
- **British control:** Philadelphia fell to British soldiers near the end of 1777, and then in early 1778 the British left as they marched to attack and capture New York.
- **US Constitution:** Written in Philadelphia in 1787, the US Constitution was influenced by Penn and his laws that made Pennsylvania what it was.
- **US Mint:** When Congress passed the Coinage Act in 1792, the first city to have a mint was Philadelphia.
- **US Capital:** Philadelphia would even be the nation's capital (1790–1800), an honor that only a few other US cities hold.
- **Susan B. Anthony:** Born in a Quaker family and educated in a Quaker school near Philadelphia, Susan B. Anthony fought for the abolition of slavery as well as the right of women to vote. She famously spoke from outside Independence Hall in Philadelphia. The US dollar coin (1979–1981, 1999) bears her likeness. The Philadelphia mint was one of the two mints that did her coin.

66 If we would amend the world we should mend ourselves; and teach our children to be, not what we are, but what they should be. 99

– WILLIAM PENN

Benjamin Franklin moved to Philadelphia in 1723 (at age 17) and would go on to leave a permanent mark on the city. He helped establish the first hospital, fire station, and public library in Philadelphia decades before the United States was born.

But there was more. The Colony of Pennsylvania hired Franklin in 1757 to go to England and argue against the Penn family. You see, the Penn family still had legal ownership of Pennsylvania, which meant they could nix laws they didn't like and, most importantly, they did not have to pay any taxes.

Remember the 25,000,000 acres the Penn family had? Penn was able to sell less than one million acres, which meant they still owned more than 24,000,000 acres, which was about 95 percent of the land. No wonder they sent Franklin to England!

Most likely, Franklin met and argued with the Penn brothers during the five years that he was there, but unfortunately for Franklin and the Colony of Pennsylvania, the Crown sided with the Penns.

The Penn family would eventually lose Pennsylvania, but it would take many years and the defeat of the British Empire before it happened.

If I could spend time with William Penn, I would ask him a million questions, including:

1. You experienced great pain and loss, abandonment, even imprisonment. What's your secret for moving on when everything seems to be going wrong around you?

2. You wrote a lot, with more than 40 books and pamphlets under your name. One of your most famous books, *No Cross, No Crown,* was written in 1669 while you were in prison. What made that book so special?

3. You saw the need for freedom of religion long before others did. What do you think would have happened to England if they had simply allowed all of you (Quakers, Pilgrims, and other denominations) who left the country in search of religious freedom to stay?

America would not be what it is today if it had not been for people like William Penn. He left a lasting imprint on Pennsylvania and the people who lived there, and that, in turn, benefited the nation, especially during its formative years.

William Penn
1644–1718

Benjamin Franklin
1706–1790

Though Benjamin Franklin was 12 years old when William Penn died in England, he moved to Penn's city of Philadelphia when he was 17 years old. He made it his home and brought great value to the city. He knew Penn's sons and probably met them while arguing against the Penn family in British courts. He would end up being buried in Philadelphia.

CHAPTER 4

Benjamin Franklin

1706–1790

You may know Benjamin Franklin as the face on the US $100 bill, one of the Founding Fathers, or the crazy guy who flew a kite in a storm to prove that lightning was actually electricity.

He also happened to be the only person to sign the Declaration of Independence, the Treaty of Alliance with France, the Treaty of Paris, and the US Constitution!

But there is a lot more to Ben Franklin.

Born in Boston, Massachusetts, in 1706, he was number 15 of 17 children. Families were big back then, but that's still a lot of kids! Four of his siblings died in childhood, including the two right before him, and he ended up outliving all his siblings.

Franklin had very little formal education, and what he did have consisted of about two years of grammar, writing, and arithmetic. For the most part, he schooled himself by being a voracious reader, writing extensively, and debating with other people. He continued this habit for the rest of his life, and it enabled him to mingle with the brightest minds of his time.

In fact, Franklin went on to be a recognized inventor, Postmaster of Philadelphia, and the first Postmaster General. He also established Philadelphia's first police force and fire department, started the American Philosophical Society and the Pennsylvania Hospital, and founded the University of Pennsylvania and Franklin and Marshall College.

Not bad for the lowly, uneducated son of a Boston candle and soap maker!

Early to Bed, Early to Rise

At the age of 10, Franklin went to work in his father's shop. Becoming a preacher was his father's wish, but young Franklin had always wanted to be a sailor. They met somewhere in the middle on that, and Franklin's father arranged for him to be an apprentice and learn the printing trade from his older brother, James, who ran a print shop.

While working with his brother, who had founded the *New England Courant* weekly newspaper, Franklin discovered a way to make his own voice heard. He would slip anonymous essays under the shop door at night, which his brother would read and then publish. Franklin wasn't even 16 years old yet, and already he had thoughts and opinions that were valuable enough for society to read them.

Those essays might have included some of these or similar words of wisdom:

- "Early to bed and early to rise makes a man healthy, wealthy, and wise."
- "Glass, china, and reputation are easily cracked and never well mended."
- "Lost time is never found again."
- "An investment in knowledge pays the best interest."
- "No gains without pains."
- "Well done is better than well said."
- "He who lies down with dogs shall rise up with fleas."

Witty though they are, these quotes by Benjamin Franklin show a depth of truth that benefits both character and community alike.

He used to say that a secret can only be held by three people if two of them are dead. He kept it secret that he was the one submitting these anonymous essays to his brother for more than 50 years, only telling when his autobiography was published.

Franklin must have felt stifled or bored, for he quit, at age 17, his apprenticeship with his brother and fled to start his own life in Philadelphia. Naturally, he landed a job at a printing press. While there, he wrote a letter to his parents explaining where he was.

Somehow, the governor, William Keith, happened to read it. He was so impressed with Franklin that he promised to set him up as an independent printer. He sent Franklin to London to secure supplies and promised a letter of introduction to precede him there.

Maybe it was Franklin's drive, his passion, his way with words, or something else, but Franklin was only 18 years old at the time!

Off to England

Unfortunately, the governor (who had a history of "forgetting" things) forgot to send his letter of introduction (or never intended to), and Franklin arrived in London empty-handed and with no one knowing he was coming.

I don't know about you, but that would have made me go crazy! Just imagine traveling 3,000 miles by boat to buy materials for a business the governor sent you to do but didn't bother to make sure the avenues to acquire those materials were in place!

Doubly unfortunate, Franklin later found that the governor had changed his mind (or again, never intended to) and was not going to set Franklin up as an independent printer.

66 Honesty is the best policy. 99

– BENJAMIN FRANKLIN

It didn't seem to trouble Franklin. Within a few days, he had a job with one of the most famous printers in London.

He ended up working in London for a year and a half. His earnings provided food and lodging, as well as pay for his return passage.

When the day came to leave, Franklin could look back on his time with a real sense of accomplishment. He had turned a very bad situation into a very good one, had networked with many influential people in London, and had gained enough experience to launch his own business upon his return home.

Only in hindsight can some things be seen, and that is certainly the case with Franklin. His future role with England and Europe, and his role with the United States, benefited greatly by this year and a half that he spent in England.

It took weeks to cross the Atlantic back in those days, so Franklin had plenty of time to think and write on the voyage home. He used his time wisely and penned a set of standards to live by. These weren't just any list of character traits or skills to have. His set of standards would become the basis of how he would help craft the Constitution of the United States!

Upon returning to Pennsylvania, he promptly founded his own printing shop and newspaper, the *Pennsylvania Gazette*. It was an immediate success. He even printed a novel, *Pamela*, which would end up being the first novel to be printed in America.

Marriage and Family

This is where, on the personal front, things got really complicated for Franklin. Before he left for England, he had proposed to Deborah Read, but her mother would not allow it due to his pending trip to England and overall lack of money.

While he was in England, Deborah was pushed into marriage, but her husband ended up being a loser. Within six months, he spent her dowry, ran up debts, couldn't hold a job, and ran off with a slave to the Caribbean islands where he apparently was killed, though nobody knows for sure.

Finally, in 1730, Deborah married Ben Franklin, but it was a common-law marriage because Deborah could not officially be divorced from her first husband, and nobody knew if he was dead or not.

But this is where it gets even more complicated. You see, Franklin had been unfaithful himself, siring a child (William Franklin) that same year with an unknown woman.

Deborah agreed to adopt the baby and would eventually have two other children with Franklin: Francis (1732) and Sarah (1743).

Sadly, Francis died of smallpox as a child. This loss, it is said, left a gaping hole in Franklin's heart from which he never fully recovered.

Franklin turned his sorrow into productivity. He pushed himself to do more and achieve more, even becoming a staple of Philadelphia's civic life. This was when he helped create the first hospital, fire station, and police force in Philadelphia.

Business Is Booming

Whether it was a purposeful strategy or an accidental by-product, Franklin created associations and partnerships that could operate independently yet allow him to use his influence for the benefit of society. He established more connections in the printing world all along the eastern coast. He owned a stake in them and handled their supplies. This gave him tremendous reach, much like a franchise today across many industries.

In Philadelphia, he created a post office to meet the city's needs, using it also to help distribute his own newspaper.

Just like today, any successful person will have detractors. There were some who didn't care for Franklin and thought he was just out to make a quick buck on the backs of the middle class. (Sound familiar?)

But contrary to those who opposed him, Franklin was a pretty normal guy who preferred, as the popular saying of his time was, a "fur hat over a wig." He was a common man who rarely dressed fancy and who didn't parade his accomplishments around. After all, his epitaph excluded most of his professions and simply read, "Printer."

With businesses set up and things in place, Franklin began to spend more time on his inventions. Electricity fascinated him, and so began his quest of understanding electricity and attempting to store it. The major hurdle was that he didn't really know how it worked. There was no universal principle to it because the standard definition of what electricity was hadn't been invented yet. At that time, a huge swath of the population still believed it was a direct action of God himself and not a scientific concept.

> 66 To succeed, jump as quickly at opportunities as you do at conclusions. 99
>
> – BENJAMIN FRANKLIN

In pursuit of this, Franklin established the general physical rules of electricity. He gave us terms like "positive" and "negative" to describe electricity and coined the term "battery." He conducted his famous kite-and-key experiment in a lightning storm in 1752. His daughter, Sarah, was nine years old at the time. Maybe he told her about it or maybe she was even there. We'll never know.

Back then, people had no concept of electricity beyond static electricity and its blue arc that appeared when zapping each other's ears after shuffling around in a sweater.

Franklin not only studied electricity, he also tried to store it. Today, we can buy batteries almost anywhere, pop them in a flashlight, and have instant electricity and light! These concepts were black magic back in Franklin's time. In fact, clergymen condemned him for the thought that lightning was anything but God's way of striking down sinners, even after the science was independently confirmed by other scientists in France.

He would travel back and forth to England many times prior to the American Revolution. He was well respected there for his science, inventions, and witty conversations. A few of his inventions include:

1. The Franklin Stove—countless homes have been kept warm by Franklin's more efficient stove.
2. Bifocals—he needed them, and millions of other people over the centuries have as well.
3. The lightning rod—to pull electricity away from the house and drive it into the ground, thus saving countless homes from catching fire.
4. Swim fins—he first made them as a boy to help him swim faster.
5. A flexible urinary catheter—his brother needed this, so he created one and immediately sent it to him.
6. The Armonica—this musical instrument was vastly improved over other versions.

To come up with such a diverse set of inventions shows me that Franklin's mind was always exposed to new things. (To me, he was the Elon Musk of his time.) Franklin experimented here, traveled there, tried this, improved that, never limiting himself by thinking, "I'm not allowed to do this" or "I'm not able to do that." He simply did it. I really respect that.

If I could ask Franklin something, I would ask him three things:

First, describe your mindset. How do you think? What habits do you have that enable you to accomplish all that you do each day?

Second, you obviously loved the 13 Colonies. What did you see that might help us today? What should we do with anti-Americans who are in positions of power?

Third, what was the true intention of the Second Amendment? Would you have ever intended people to be required to get a permit to carry? Would you ban AR-15s?

I could pepper him with questions for hours, but I am eternally grateful that he was one of our Founding Fathers.

What many people probably don't know is that Franklin was gone for extended periods of time, seven years one time and ten another. He invited Deborah to join him when he was in England, but each time she refused. They corresponded regularly with letters, which meant at least six to eight weeks to get a reply to any questions asked.

While on one of his extended trips in England, his wife, Deborah, died from a stroke in 1774. She was buried in Philadelphia (at the Christ Church Burial Ground), and Franklin would eventually be laid beside her when he died 16 years later.

But those next 16 years would see the birth of a nation, with Benjamin Franklin there shepherding every step of the way.

Diving into Politics

Franklin was involved in politics long before he was himself a focal point of it. As a printer and founder of a newspaper, whether he knew it or not, had been a player in the game from a young age. He even used his press to print money for Delaware and Pennsylvania. Like others in the printing industry, they were often more knowledgeable on a political subject than the politicians themselves. In fact, Franklin was probably more well-read on all subjects of his day than anyone else around him. It wasn't until later in life that he more actively used his knowledge and influence in politics.

> 66 We must, indeed, all hang together or, most assuredly, we shall all hang separately. 99
>
> – Benjamin Franklin

The Colonies were going through changes, especially in relation to England. It was the Stamp Act of 1765, a tax by Great Britain on anything printed in the Colonies, that first made him realize that the Colonies were destined for war with England.

Riots and protests erupted in the Colonies. The Stamp Act was part of the infamous battle cry of the Colonists for "No taxation without representation."

Realizing that the Stamp Act was hurting the relationship of Great Britain with the Colonies, Franklin went to the House of Commons in England and petitioned to repeal it.

His speech garnered him significant favorability back in the Colonies, but the British snubbed their noses at him. They wanted to maintain power and continue the revenue stream with taxes.

The conflict reached a boiling point shortly after. When Franklin heard about the Boston Tea Party, he knew war was inevitable.

Franklin had been serving as representative for diplomacy to London for several Colonies, advocating heavily for more independent governance. But when he published certain letters by the Massachusetts Governor Thomas Hutchinson in the *Boston Gazette*, some questioned Franklin's loyalties. The published letters recommended strong repressive measures against anyone who defied the Crown in the Colonies. This only made the Colonists angrier, and they demanded Hutchinson's removal.

In this case, for highlighting the truth, distributing the letters, showing the governor's support for the crown, and exposing hypocrisy, Franklin was the one who received punishment! Does that sound familiar?

Called in front of a British hearing, Franklin was berated as disloyal and called a common thief for simply publishing the words of the Massachusetts governor. His role as Postmaster General was immediately revoked.

This was Franklin's turning point and likely the basis for the First Amendment. He had entered that room as a loyal British servant, but he left as a patriot ready for war.

When he finally arrived back in Philadelphia in 1775, everything had changed. Deborah had been buried almost six months earlier, war with England was the subject of almost every conversation, and a warrant had been issued for his arrest!

Benjamin Franklin was now a revolutionary hero.

He was then sent as a delegate to the Second Continental Congress and appointed to draft the Declaration of Independence. He took the job seriously, joining with Thomas Jefferson and others, to explain the rights held by every human being.

Remember Franklin's illegitimate son, William? He grew up and followed his father into politics, but unlike his father, William maintained an unwavering allegiance to the Crown. When Franklin returned to Philadelphia, William was governor of New Jersey. It was literally father against son.

The Revolutionary War

The day Congress adopted the Declaration of Independence, Franklin was 70 years old with kidney stones, gout, and other health problems, but he was already in France, working to help the Colonies in their struggle for independence.

Many people don't know this, but Franklin was in France during the Revolutionary War actively working to provide George Washington's army with the supplies he needed to fight the British. Franklin's experience and skills in trading, networking, organizing, and communicating all came into play at a truly pivotal time.

Some accused him of hiding in France, but Franklin worked tirelessly as the first American ambassador to help the Colonies. He was the premier negotiator in France for arms and goods that helped us win the Revolutionary War. Without him, our soldiers would not have had the resources to fight.

He was the OG arms dealer, if you will.

Prior to signing the Treaty of Paris in 1783, which officially ended the Revolutionary War, Franklin was tasked with negotiating a peace agreement with England that included their alliance with France. Not exactly an easy thing to do!

In the spring of 1785, at 79 years old, Franklin returned home. Then in 1787, he would be the oldest delegate sent to Philadelphia to help craft and sign the US Constitution.

> 66 The Constitution only gives people the right to pursue happiness. You have to catch it yourself. 99
>
> – BENJAMIN FRANKLIN

Before the signing of the Constitution, Franklin gave a speech where he noted that while he may not agree with everything now, it didn't mean he would not agree with it later. He was essentially saying that perfection was the enemy of progress. (Good advice for us to always consider!) He encouraged everybody to sign the Constitution despite personal reservations against individual aspects of it. For this, he was known as the Unifier.

Regarding the Constitution, Franklin later said, "Our new Constitution is now established, everything seems to promise it will be durable; but, in this world, nothing is certain except death and taxes."

Franklin's health declined through the last few years of his life. Sarah, his daughter, took care of him and was with him when he died. More than 20,000 people came to his funeral.

Always having a way with words, Franklin wrote his own epitaph at age 22, many years prior to his death. Knowing he was an author, publisher, and printer, his words were perfect:

The Body of B. Franklin, Printer
Like the Cover of an old Book
Its Contents torn out,
And stript of its Lettering and Gilding,
Lies here, Food for Worms,
But the Work shall not be wholly lost:
For it will, as he believ'd,
Appear once more
In a new & more perfect Edition,
Corrected and amended by the Author.

Benjamin Franklin 1706–1790		**George Washington** 1732–1805

Benjamin Franklin knew George Washington well and was quick to nominate him to fight the British, but what made them blood-brothers was their firmly held belief that the British no longer had the right to control them, tax them, or decide their future. They demanded independence and were willing to die fighting for it.

CHAPTER 5

George Washington

1732–1805

When most people think about American history, the first name that comes to mind is often George Washington. And rightfully so, for General George Washington led a grossly outnumbered and outgunned civilian militia against the most powerful military in the world at that time . . . and won!

It was the American Revolution, and if it were not for George Washington, I don't know if we would have won the war with England. Maybe later, years later, but Washington was the right man in the right place at the right time.

As you might expect for a fighter like Washington, his early life was not so easy. He had to work hard and keep working, take risks (including his own life), lead boldly even when he was sick, take responsibility for problems not his own, pay for things he shouldn't have had to pay for, and move forward under bitter disappointment.

Life wasn't easy, but he made it what it was.

Washington's successes are outstanding for any person, more so given some of the challenges he faced. Most psychologists and guidance counselors today would probably predict a grim future for him and would certainly never have predicted that he would be one of the Founding Fathers, if not *the* Founding Father of this country.

Washington the Soldier

While Washington was born in the colonies in 1732 and never knew much of England firsthand, he still aspired to the structure of British culture. His family was moderately wealthy, owning a series of farms in Virginia, but when Washington was 11, his father died.

At his father's death, young Washington became the ward of his older half brother, Lawrence. It was Lawrence who inherited the family estates, and it was Lawrence who built the famous house and named the property Mount Vernon.

Washington gained much from Lawrence, including further education, manners, social life, and a network of friends who would benefit him in other ways. One neighbor and relative of Lawrence's wife kept teenage Washington very busy as a land surveyor.

Because of his father's death and despite Lawrence's help, Washington was still mostly self-educated. He had the basics of reading, writing, and arithmetic as a child, but little formal schooling prior to age 15. Beyond that, he was self-taught.

Think about that for a minute. Being self-taught is no easy task. How many 15-year-olds today are disciplined enough to continue their own education to the level high enough to hold a job, let alone become a national influence? Sadly, we have teens today who eat Tide pods.

In 1752, Lawrence died of tuberculosis. Washington and his mother were left to care for the estate, along with the slaves the family owned. (Yes, the family had owned slaves for many years, but that doesn't mean Washington must be wiped from the history books as if he never existed.)

After Lawrence's death, Washington enlisted in the British militia at age 20. His father and grandfather, as well as Lawrence, had all served, and Washington wanted to do likewise.

At age 21, Washington was sent by Virginia's lieutenant governor on a diplomatic mission to tell the French in Ohio to stop taking land claimed by the British.

Now just to put this in perspective, when I was 21, I enlisted to become a Navy SEAL. I was the second most junior enlisted rank, and I'm telling you, I was certainly not on the short list for any lieutenant governors to carry a diplomatic message that could potentially spark a war between nations.

Only a special type of person, especially at age 21, would be given that much trust and responsibility.

When Washington arrived, the French basically told him to go pound sand. They were not leaving, nor had they any intention of leaving.

> 66 Leadership is not only having a vision, but also having the courage, the discipline, and the resources to get you there. 99
>
> – GEORGE WASHINGTON

Washington left, narrowly missed being shot by an Indian, and returned to Williamsburg, Virginia. The lieutenant governor promptly sent Washington back (as a lieutenant colonel) with about 150 men to attack the French.

For those in the know, it is staggering to imagine a 23-year-old lieutenant colonel! Today, most lieutenants colonels are at least 10 years older than Washington was.

Surprising a detachment of 30 French soldiers and killing the commander, they were able to move forward and even take the French fort. Their success was short-lived, for the French besieged the fort soon after with superior forces and took Washington and many of his men captive.

The men were disarmed and allowed to return to Virginia, on the condition that the British stay away and not build another fort for a year. Despite the loss, Washington's courage, leadership, and valor earned him praise back in London, and he was promoted to colonel.

With that battle, the French and Indian War had begun, and Washington had played a significant role in starting it.

Remember, Washington was still only 23 years old, not even old enough to get a rental car without a surcharge these days, yet he could command troops for key critical battles with global implications.

Ignoring the 12-month leave-us-alone request by the French, England sent a much larger British force to retake the French fort, this time under the command of General Edward Braddock.

Washington had grown frustrated with the British army. Their lack of support and illogical chain of command offended him so much that he briefly retired from the Virginia militia. But when Braddock expressed his appreciation for all that Washington had done, Washington agreed to join Braddock as his personal aide-de-camp. It was an unpaid position, but Washington was back to fighting, which he had found to be of his liking.

Along the way, the British forces were ambushed. In the fighting, Washington had two horses shot out from under him and had four bullet holes through his jacket. General Braddock was mortally wounded, but before he died, he appointed Washington to be Commander-in-Chief of all the Virginia forces.

Though the British lost the battle, Washington's decisive tactics were credited with avoiding what could have been a catastrophic loss of lives and resources.

Upon his return to Virginia, Washington's distaste for his role in the military grew by the treatment he received from senior members of the British military, many of whom had never seen battle. His colonist soldiers were considered inferior to the British officers, even though many had much more experience and greater skill.

> " A pack of jackasses led by a lion is superior to a pack of lions led by a jackass. "
>
> – GEORGE WASHINGTON

What's more, he became increasingly frustrated with the caliber of men who were being assigned to him. They were undisciplined, often drunk, and not fully committed to the cause. It also didn't help that the colonial legislature had very little commitment to properly outfitting his army, much less providing logistical support.

He was basically trying to run an entire state's militia with a bunch of farmers and craftsmen whose focus was on making it home alive to their families.

Armed with new orders from England, Washington and his men marched out to fight the French again, but this time, the French abandoned and burned the fort before the British arrived.

When he returned this time, Washington asked for a regular commission, just as his half brother Lawrence had received. All the good he had done, as well as promises from General Braddock, landed on deaf ears. Washington was denied his commission. He was furious!

I can imagine him walking out of there with an "I'll show them!" attitude. Eventually, he would get his chance.

This time, he resigned for good from the British militia. After years of fighting on behalf of a monarch thousands of miles away, he had very little to show for it.

In January 1759, he penned this letter to the officers he served with:

"Permit me then to conclude with the following acknowledgments: first, that I always thought it, as it really was, the greatest honor of my life to command Gentlemen, who made me happy in their company & easy by their conduct: secondly, that had everything contributed as fully as your obliging endeavours did to render me satisfied, I never should have been otherwise, or have had cause to know the pangs I have felt at parting with a Regiment, that has shared my toils, and experienced every hardship & danger, which I have encountered. But this brings on reflections that fill me with grief & I must strive to forget them; in thanking you, Gentlemen, with uncommon sincerity & true affection for the honor you have done me—for if I have acquired any reputation, it is from you I derive it."[2]

Washington the Farmer

As soon as Washington resigned, he married Martha Dandridge, a widow with two children, whom he had proposed to several months earlier. He focused on farming and taking care of his estate. He had thousands of acres, plus thousands more from his wife, and he proved to be a doting father, as well as an excellent land manager.

For the next 15 years, up until the American Revolution, he was very busy with everything that a big landowner had to deal with: building, crops, crop rotation, making and growing the necessary items, ordering supplies from England as needed, and much more. He also served as Justice of the Peace in his county of Fairfax.

As a farmer, Washington understood the very real impact of confiscation by the government via taxes. Already soured to the British system after being denied a commission, he was doubly incensed by the increasing burden of taxes. He penned a letter to George Mason in April of 1769:

[2] https://founders.archives.gov/documents/Washington/02-06-02-0152

"At a time when our lordly Masters in Great Britain will be satisfied with nothing less than the deprivation of American freedom, it seems highly necessary that something shou'd be done to avert the stroke and maintain the liberty which we have derived from our Ancestors; but the manner of doing it to answer the purpose effectually is the point in question."[3]

Tensions mounted as the British government imposed more taxes and acted more tyrannically toward the colonists. The Stamp Act of 1765, the Townsend Acts of 1767–68, and the Tea Act of 1773 imposed greater taxes and limited commerce. The Boston Massacre in 1770 resulted in the deaths of colonists as the British soldiers opened fire on what they perceived to be a mob.

These actions led the colonists to "celebrate" with the Boston Tea Party in 1773, where they threw British tea into Boston Harbor.

Knowing that the increase in tension might lead to accusations of sedition and further oppressive responses by Britain, Washington appealed to the Crown for more rational taxation policies.

As you know, the King of England did not listen.

On the night of April 18th, 1775, hundreds of British troops marched the 20 miles from Boston to Concord, Massachusetts, to seize the militia's arms supply. This is when Paul Revere made his famous ride, alerting the militia that "The British are coming."

The next day was the "Shot heard round the world" at the battle of Lexington and Concord. The revolution had officially begun!

[3] https://founders.archives.gov/documents/Washington/02-08-02-0132

In response, Washington reportedly wrote in his letter to George William Fairfax on May 31, 1775:

"Unhappy it is though to reflect, that a Brother's Sword has been sheathed in a Brother's breast, and that, the once happy and peaceful plains of America are either to be drenched with Blood, or Inhabited by Slaves. Sad alternative! But can a virtuous Man hesitate in his choice?"[4]

66 Occupants of public offices love power and are prone to abuse it. 99

– GEORGE WASHINGTON

Less than a month later, the Continental Army would taste its first defeat at the Battle of Bunker Hill. This emboldened the newly formed Continental Army with a new motivation.

Almost simultaneously, the Second Continental Congress commissioned Washington as the Commander in Chief of the Continental Army.

I am sure the British were thinking to themselves, "We should have commissioned this dude for our team when we had the chance!"

They would never get the chance again. On July 4th, 1776, the Continental Congress voted to adopt the Declaration of Independence.

---

[4] https://founders.archives.gov/documents/Washington/02-10-02-0281

Through the rest of the year, it seemed to be an almost certain loss for the colonies. The British sent more than thousands of troops to push Washington and his forces back. It wasn't until a secret crossing of the Delaware River on Christmas night, that led to a decisive military victory by Washington's men, that the morale shifted for the Colonists.

You have no doubt seen pictures of Washington crossing the river in the ice and snow, but I want you to really grasp the fighting spirit of the grossly outnumbered and outgunned newly formed American army. Many of those men had gone months without a proper meal, they lacked adequate clothing, some didn't even have shoes, and they all suffered multiple defeats up to that point.

This puts things into perspective for our current increasingly politicized military today. I can't help but wonder:

Do we still have the guts, drive, and determination to be like George Washington? I hope so, but when character, strength, and skill are no longer prized, I can't help but wonder.

With Washington, there were many battles where he was on the front lines. He was not sitting behind his desk somewhere safe and away from harm. Wherever the action was, Washington was right there in the middle of it. I can't help but believe:

If our current military leaders made decisions from the front lines, much better decisions would be made. We could easily avoid catastrophic decisions, such as the multi-billion-dollar Afghanistan withdrawal fiasco.

While not diminishing the remainder of Washington's war efforts over the next few years that resulted in this young nation winning the war against the much older and more experienced England, it wasn't until 1783 and the Treaty of Paris that the American Revolution would be over.

Washington the President

At the end of the American Revolution, Washington promptly gave up his command, returning the power back to the people.

He then returned to Mount Vernon, probably expecting to quietly enjoy retirement and live the rest of his life in the beauty and solitude of his family estate.

But that would not be. Everyone needed him, especially the country.

Only a few years later, he was called upon to attend the Constitutional Convention in the summer of 1787 in Philadelphia and to head the committee to draft our Constitution.

Mind you, Washington was 55 years old at this point. For us today, Mount Vernon in Virginia to Philadelphia, Pennsylvania, is a quick train or car ride, but back then, the 260-mile journey would have taken most of a week. That would tire anyone out.

And then when the first American presidential election was held on January 7, 1789, Washington was unanimously elected our first president.

He was at the helm as the new country with a new form of government struggled forward. While in office, he commissioned

America's capitol on the Potomac River that was appropriately named after him.

> 66 The marvel of all history is the patience with which men and women submit to burdens unnecessarily laid upon them by their governments. 99
>
> – GEORGE WASHINGTON

Because there was no real precedent set in this form of governance in the history of mankind, Washington lived by a few key tenets:

- fairness
- prudence
- integrity

If everyone in any public office today, in any country around the world, would heed these simple three choices, it would revolutionize everything!

Very interestingly, especially considering today's weak-kneed cancel culture climate, Washington was known for nominating people who disagreed with him because it would spur debate and produce better results. He did this with Thomas Jefferson and Alexander Hamilton.

Can you imagine some of the debates that might have gone on as they crafted our Republic? I can see James Madison and others sitting there thinking:

"So, we are going to give everyone the right to say whatever they want AND we are going to make sure everyone can have a gun too. This country is going to be awesome!"

Most of all, Washington implemented the spirit of the Declaration of Independence, the Constitution, and the Bill or Rights into an actual government.

That was a feat very few people in all of history could have accomplished.

Washington was nothing less than a miracle in the history of this country. And yet, some people today want him washed from our history books because he was a warrior, a slave owner, and even (according to the British) a traitor.

But without George Washington, those same disagreeable people might not have the freedom to publish that opinion, would still answer to a monarch over 3,000 miles away, and would not live in this great country.

As Ronald Reagan said:

"If we look to the answer as to why for so many years we achieved so much, prospered as no other people on earth, it was because here in this land we unleashed the energy and individual genius of man to a greater extent than has ever been done before. Freedom and the dignity of the individual have been more available and assured here than in any other place on earth. The price for this freedom at times has been high, but we have never been unwilling to pay that price."

If I could ask Washington something, I would ask him three things:

First, you never stopped. What drove you to keep fighting for this country, regardless of the seemingly impossible odds?

Second, you took a lot of risks, especially in war. Were you simply young and brash, or did you fully believe that God would protect you if it was meant to be?

Third, what would you say to the people of today? In many ways, our own government has taxed us and treated us like England did before the Revolution. What advice would you give us?

George Washington may have had no biological children of his own, but in my books, he is the father of this great country. And for that, we all owe him a debt of gratitude.

George Washington **John Adams**
1732–1805   1735–1826

John Adams was George Washington's vice president. They were both pioneers and both US presidents. They shared a gift—the ability to function while surrounded by vast amounts of chaos—and they shared an unwavering love for this country.

CHAPTER 6

John Adams

1735-1826

Born in 1735, John Adams played a pivotal role in American history, including but not limited to the following:

- He pressed for American independence.
- He wrote the constitution for the state of Massachusetts, which was then used as a model for other states.
- He was a signer of the Treaty of Paris in 1783.
- He was the first vice president of the United States.

- He was the second president of the United States.
- His son, John Quincy Adams, became the sixth president.

Adams's father wanted him to be a minister. After all, his family could trace their Christian roots back to the original Pilgrims who had come to these shores on the *Mayflower.*

So, at the young age of 16, Adams attended Harvard on a scholarship to do just that. After graduation, he was a schoolteacher for several years, but his interests were in law. Back to school he went, this time to become a lawyer.

Little did he know that his legal skills would play such an important role in the Colonies and their eventual struggle for independence.

A few days before his 29th birthday, he married Abigail Smith, a minister's daughter. She was no ordinary woman and would prove to be the perfect match for him in every position he held.

> 66 One useless man is a shame, two is a law firm, and three is a Congress. 99
>
> – JOHN ADAMS

They would have six children, but one died in infancy and one was stillborn. Their second child, John Quincy, would follow his dad's footsteps to France, to law school, and to the US presidency (the sixth president).

On the home front, Abigail was left to manage most everything, especially the house and land, as Adams would spend less and less time at home, as his legal practice and then politics kept him away.

The Stamp Act of 1765 made almost everyone in the Colonies mad enough to throw all of England's tea into the ocean, though the Boston Tea Party wouldn't happen for another eight years.

Adams was a stark opponent to the Stamp Act. Knowing how to reach the masses, he published four articles in the *Boston Gazette* opposing the Stamp Act. He then denounced it in a speech to the Massachusetts governor, saying that it was invalid and therefore could not be enforced.

At the time, it was a shock for anyone to give such a speech because expressing open opposition to the British government could result in charges of treason, and that meant death. The government had unilateral control over punishment.

Interestingly, this very lack of freedom (expressing open opposition) was so important to Adams and other Founding Fathers that they were sure to include freedom of speech in the Bill of Rights.

Innocent Until Proven Guilty

Adams was a just man and he believed that everyone had the right to representation and a fair trial. To not only prove his point, but to also do what he felt was right, he volunteered in 1770 to represent the British soldiers who had shot and killed civilians in what would be called the Boston Massacre.

Naturally, public opinion ran against the soldiers, but Adams argued that they were innocent until proven guilty.

Adams took his role as advocate very seriously, and despite his desire for independence from Great Britain, he argued that it was not a case of British vs. Colonist but of human vs. human. He even asked the jury what they would have done if they were in the soldiers' shoes.

Adam's argument, approach, and earth-shattering perspective would become the basis of our legal system in America.

He took a great risk in being the defense lawyer for the British soldiers, and he was denounced for it by many colonists, but he also gained respect and notoriety among others for his fair and honest treatment.

Adams was a man of just character, and he proved it, time and time again.

Soon after, Adams was elected to the Massachusetts Assembly and chosen to represent the colony at the First Continental Congress in 1774. In 1775, Adams was one of the first to nominate George Washington as Commander in Chief of the Continental Army.

Adams laid the framework for the notion that each colony should form an independent government, and later pushed for the respect of the 10th Amendment. When he seconded Richard Henry Lee's motion for independence, Adams was one of the five men chosen to draft the Declaration of Independence.

In 1779, he was sent to meet Ben Franklin to negotiate the Treaty of Paris and would remain in France until 1785 while negotiating trade deals with much of Europe. Subsequently, in 1785, he became the first US Minister to England.

Much like Ben Franklin, America might not have survived its battle for independence had not John Adams helped to secure the international trade and structure that he did.

66 But a Constitution of Government once changed from Freedom, can never be restored. Liberty, once lost, is lost forever. 99

– John Adams

After spending nearly a decade in Europe, Adams returned to America. The length of time he and many other politicians spent abroad is staggering by today's standards. Don't forget, they had no phones, faxes, or internet, which meant that all business was conducted by mail or in person, and that was always by boat. It would take weeks if not months to correspond, let alone have all the facts so you could make decisions.

Soon after his return, on February 4, 1789, the first presidential election of the United States was held. All 69 electors gathered to cast their ballots for the presidency, and each elector could cast two votes.

All 69 electors cast one vote for Washington, who won unanimously. When the second votes for various other candidates were counted, Adams had received 34 of them, which made him the first vice president of the United States!

Then in 1796, after Washington decided not to run for a third term, Adams was elected president as Washington's successor, with Thomas Jefferson as the vice president.

During his time in office, things became heated with France. Would it be war or peace? The new nation could not sustain another war on the heels of its recent revolution, so Adams went the extra mile to maintain peace. This choice was a good move for the nation, but it cost him politically.

This took incredible nerve and self-confidence. But I like that about Adams. He had the guts to do what was right rather than what was popular. Most politicians today are more concerned about reelection than they are about the people and country they serve. That is small-minded as well as incredibly selfish.

Adams did what was right, just as he did when he defended the British soldiers of the Boston Massacre. Both the United States and France benefited from his selfless choice, but he lost out. When it came time for reelection, Jefferson won. Adams was relieved of duty.

Life After Presidency

I think Adams was very relieved when he was not voted in for a second term, for he and Abigail left the White House (they were the first to live in it) and headed back home to Quincy, Massachusetts, even before the inauguration of Thomas Jefferson!

For 25 more years, Adams wrote extensively, especially in letters to Thomas Jefferson, about politics, America, religion, history, and life. Abigail would pass away in 1818 from typhoid fever and would be buried there in Quincy. Eight years later, Adams would be laid to rest beside her.

I always found it interesting that the last words by Adams were, "Thomas Jefferson survives." But he did not know, as they had no telephone, that Jefferson had died just five to six hours before at his home in Virginia.

> " I pray Heaven to bestow the best of Blessings on this House and all that shall hereafter inhabit it. May none but honest and wise Men ever rule under this roof. "

> — JOHN ADAMS, IN A LETTER TO HIS WIFE, WRITTEN THE SECOND NIGHT AT THE NEWLY BUILT WHITE HOUSE

John Adams and Thomas Jefferson had been close friends, then bitter rivals, and then close friends once again after extensive correspondence between the two of them. They were some of the most prominent, and almost the longest living Founding Fathers, who had helped create this country.

They both died on July 4, 1826. It was the 50th anniversary of the Declaration of Independence, which they both had signed.

If I could ask Adams anything, I would ask him these four questions:

1. You spent years studying European politics and European history, trying to find principles and truths that could be applied to our new government. What advice would you give our president, our Senate, and our Congress today?

2. You tried to always do what was right, even when it meant you might lose or not be so well-liked. Why would you risk it?

3. What advice would you give for people struggling with forgiveness? You and Thomas Jefferson worked things out, and for years thereafter, you both benefited because of it.

4. You spent a lot of time away from your wife and family while you worked for the US government. What advice would you give to us today who are trying to balance work, family, and life?

> 66 Those who trade liberty for security have neither. 99
>
> – JOHN ADAMS

John Adams was another Founding Father who had character as well as skill. We benefit today because of the value he brought to the table at such an important time in our history.

We also benefited from his wife, Abigail, who took a lot of verbal abuse as she stood beside her man.

Abigail Adams – First Lady Bar None!

Abigail Adams (1744–1818) married John Adams when she was 20 years old. He was 29 years old. Her father, a minister who also officiated their wedding, was not overly impressed by Adams the lawyer.

Raised to think for herself, to be well-read, and to stand by her man, Abigail did just that! She was not only Adams's wife, but she was also his advisor, confidante, family rock, and constant source of encouragement and strength.

One of my favorite exchanges between her and Adams is in one of the many letters they wrote each other, this one from 1775. Complaining that he was to be kept away for an additional month overseas, she very spiritedly wrote:

"I was pleasing myself with the thought that you would soon be upon your return. It is in vain to repine. I hope the public will reap what I sacrifice."

I don't think she took it out on the public when she became first lady (1797–1801), but she was quick-witted and had a sharp tongue. No doubt that astounded other women and probably scared a lot of men, but she would have it no other way.

Take fellow politician, Albert Gallatin, for instance. He did a great job lowering the new government's debt and helping keep the peace, especially with the Treaty of Ghent, but he was not a fan of Abigail voicing her political opinions. He later wrote, "She is Mrs. President not of the United States but of a faction . . . It is not right."

> 66 I've always felt that a person's intelligence is directly reflected by the number of conflicting points of view he can entertain simultaneously on the same topic. 99

> – ABIGAIL ADAMS

At home, she carried impossible weight. She suffered the loss of two children dying, one at birth and another in infancy. Adams wasn't even home for one of those deaths.

For the most part, she raised the children (one girl, three boys) on her own. Their son, John Quincy Adams, who would later become president, was old enough to travel to France with Adams.

Her management skills and eye for business kept the family farm going, even while they were away for extended periods of time.

As Adams's role increased in politics, Abigail's words of advice became all that more impactful. Too bad she isn't around today. She told Adams back in 1776, "If we mean to have heroes, statesmen and philosophers, we should have learned women."

I love that!

Do countries today that limit the education of their own women realize they are limiting their entire nation? Probably not, but that only makes her 250-year-old advice all that much more relevant.

Imagine having a 250-year-old answer in front of you and not applying it? That's embarrassing.

That's also true for us if we don't learn from those who have gone before us.

John and Abigail Adams held the torch of freedom incredibly high! I hope to do the same.

John Adams
1735–1826

William Clark
1770–1838

William Clark served under George Washington and probably knew John Adams personally, but it was Thomas Jefferson (as president of the United States, after he had been vice president to Adams) who was responsible for the nation's spotlight being focused on William Clark.

CHAPTER 7

William Clark

1770–1838

When John Adams left the White House, it was because his vice president, Thomas Jefferson, had been elected as the third president of the United States. One of Thomas Jefferson's greatest achievements occurred in 1803: the Louisiana Purchase.

It would make William Clark, Meriwether Lewis, and Sacajawea household names.

The Louisiana Purchase was for more land than today's state of Louisiana, which bears its name. It included land from the Gulf of Mexico (most of current-day Louisiana) west of the Mississippi to the Rocky Mountains and all the way up and beyond the Canadian border, including part or all of 15 eventual states.

That was a lot of land!

Remember how William Penn's Pennsylvania charter was about 40,000 square miles in size? Well, the Louisiana Purchase was 828,000 square miles, which is 529,920,000 acres. Jefferson paid $15 million for it, which breaks down to about three cents per acre.

I'd gladly part with $100 to get 3,333 acres. Wouldn't you?

The Louisiana Purchase doubled the size of America in one stroke of the pen. Though it cost the young nation a lot of money, it was an incredible move.

And the French were glad to sell it. They needed the money and were not doing much with the land, in part because they had just regained control of it from Spain (in 1800), it was so far from France, and because they were busy fighting their own wars in various places. This was the time of Napoleon Bonaparte, after all, and he was always fighting someone.

Most of the Louisiana Territory was still marked as "unexplored" on maps, but Jefferson had big plans for the western lands and how it might benefit the ever-expanding nation.

First, however, Jefferson needed someone to go and explore it, chart it, map it, catalogue it, touch it, and (hopefully) return with stories that would compel others to go settle there. Passage to the Pacific Ocean, possible trade, opening up the Oregon Territory, traveling routes, and knowing what and who lived there, all of it was important. Someone needed to find the answers.

As they say, if you can measure it, you can manage it. That's what Jefferson needed. But who would have the ability and the guts to try such a venture?

Lewis and Clark

President Jefferson had a personal secretary and aide-de-camp named Meriwether Lewis who seemed perfect for the job. He had been a neighbor back in Monticello, Virginia, but more importantly, he had military experience and was physically fit, smart, and well-read.

Once assigned the task, Lewis was sent to Philadelphia to learn from the brightest and best about plants and plant collection, medicine, fossils, animals, soil, astronomy, diseases, geography, and more. What they would discover during the expedition would be boxed up and sent back to Philadelphia to be studied and written about.

Lewis had served briefly in the Chosen Rifle Company, which (like its name) was a unit composed of the best riflemen around. This unit had been under the command of William Clark, who not only had years of military and leadership experience, but he also had the practical experience in the construction of forts, as well as keeping those forts supplied.

Needing help with the massive expedition and its many layers of importance, Lewis wrote to Clark and invited him to join as a copartner. And history was made. Every kid in school (at least when I was in school) grew up hearing about the legendary Lewis and Clark Expedition, and rightfully so.

Clark came from a family of soldiers and possessed the exact skills that Lewis needed to round out the team's leadership. Clark brought York, an experienced woodsman and hunter, along with him. York had been a family servant or slave on the family farm since birth. It turns out, York made quite an impact on the Indians, as they had never seen a Black man before. (Years later, it is said that Clark freed York.)

Together, Lewis and Clark planned, bought supplies, hired approximately 40 men with the necessary experience, and organized as best they could for every possible option. Going into unknown lands was bad enough, but it was the unknown Native American Indians who likely posed their greatest danger. Sure, rivers, mountains, sickness, disease, and animals were dangerous, but they don't shoot at you!

> 66 The first white men of your people who came to our country were named Lewis and Clark. 99
>
> – CHIEF JOSEPH

As for the Indians, the plan they came up with was to lead with kindness, offer gifts, be peaceful, communicate, and learn. Fighting would be out of necessity only. It would prove to be a good plan.

Imagine having to plan for a trip that would take you more than two years, traveling almost 8,000 miles by boat, horse, and on foot, into unknown terrain, weather, climates, and people.

Oh, and you have to study, document, and map everything along the way!

Not for the faint of heart!

They packed carefully, but because they had to be a little bit of everything (scientists, tradesmen, explorers, hunters, navigators, geographers, builders, soldiers, cooks, and peacekeepers), they had to take along a ton of supplies. They also had to bring gifts, such as knives, scissors, tobacco, cloth, and mirrors that could be given as gifts or traded for supplies they might need along the way.

The Lewis and Clark Expedition Begins

On May 14, 1804, the crew began their journey from St. Louis, Missouri, in their 55-foot boat. They would all return safely (except one who died from appendicitis) on September 23, 1806. What would happen between those dates would be the stuff of legends. It would also benefit our nation in countless ways, just as Jefferson had envisioned.

The city of St. Louis, which was started in the mid-1700s by the French and named after King Louis IX, sits right below the mouth of the Missouri River where it runs into the Mississippi River.

Nobody had ever followed the Missouri River to its source. That is, until the Lewis and Clark Expedition. They not only wanted to find the river's headwaters, they wanted to keep going and find passage to the Pacific Ocean.

Sailing up a river, especially a river as big as the Missouri River, is very manual. Lewis and Clark sailed if they had sufficient wind to go up faster than the river was coming down. Otherwise, they poled and pulled their way along. That is very slow going.

Almost six months later, they had reached the middle of present-day North Dakota. They had traveled 1,600 miles by boat, averaging about 10 miles a day. (Today, St. Louis to Fort Mandan by car is just over 1,000 miles, which is about a 15-hour drive.)

With winter coming, they stopped on a bend of the river and built a fort. They called it Fort Mandan after the friendly Mandan Indians who lived there. No doubt Clark's skills of fort building were put to good use.

It was here that Lewis and Clark just so happened (I see it as God's hand at work) to bump into a young Shoshone Indian woman by the name of Sacajawea, who would become their interpreter and guide, save their lives, and forever be immortalized as part of our American history.

Remember how Thomas Dermer just so happened to meet Squanto on Newfoundland Island and how, several years later, Squanto would play a vital part in the Pilgrims' survival in Plymouth? It was the same providential happenstance.

Without Sacajawea, I don't think anyone would have made it back alive from that trip. Going into hostile Indian territory without knowing the land, language, or customs was risky business.

While in Fort Mandan, they worked on their charts (Clark was the chief cartographer), continued to collect specimens, gathered food, talked with the various local Indian tribes about trade, and prepared for their trip to the Missouri River headwaters in the spring when they could travel again.

Sacajawea, just 17 years old at the time, was pregnant. Her husband, Toussaint Charbonneau of French and Indian descent, was a trapper. He had probably bought her from the Indian tribe that had kidnapped her five years earlier.

That winter, at Fort Mandan, Sacajawea gave birth to a baby boy, Jean Baptiste Charbonneau. He, too, would make his mark on American history.

Lewis and Clark identified more than 300 plants and animals over the course of their trip. A portion of those were found on the way up the Missouri and during the winter at Fort Mandan.

By the time they could resume their travels, three new members had joined the team: Sacajawea, Toussaint, and young Jean Baptiste. Sacajawea and Toussaint would prove to be invaluable interpreters and guides.

In April, the main boat returned to St. Louis with about a dozen men. On board were boxes full of samples, maps, drawings, plants, artifacts, and even a few live animals. All of it was for Thomas Jefferson and the academics back in Philadelphia.

The rest of the expedition, now just more than 30 people, went farther up the Missouri in several smaller boats and canoes. Two months later, deep into Montana up near the Canadian border, they ran into trouble. The Missouri River split into two seemingly equal parts. Which way should they go?

After scouting both rivers, they chose the southern river. It was the correct choice. Several days later, they encountered impassable water falls near present-day Great Falls, Montana.

They spent a month scouting, carrying, and walking all their stuff around the falls and back to the Missouri River. On July 4th, 1805, they were back on track.

Ahead of them they could see the Rocky Mountains. As they crossed into the mountains, the river split into three smaller rivers in today's aptly named town of Three Rivers, Montana. Lewis and Clark named the three smaller rivers in honor of those in power: Jefferson, Madison, and Gallatin.

Again, which way to go? They followed the Jefferson River, which was the most westerly of the three rivers. Again, it was the best choice, but none of the rivers would take them over the mountains or to the Pacific. They didn't know it at the time, but their plan to follow the Missouri River was about to leave them high and dry.

Amazingly, Sacajawea recognized a rock formation called Beaverhead Rock. She was back in her old homeland! Her Shoshone tribe had lived in the area, and it was from here that she had been kidnapped as a 12-year-old child.

They climbed a mountain at the present-day border of Montana and Idaho, only to see range after range beyond them. They had so far yet to go, and getting through the mountains was impossible unless you knew the way. Also, if you've ever been in the Rocky Mountains of Montana, you know it starts to get cold in August and September.

Whether they realized it or not, they were at that moment on the Continental Divide. Water flowed either east the way they had come or west toward the Pacific Ocean.

It is here that something incredible occurred. They ran into the Shoshone tribe that lived in and traveled through the area, and the leader of the Shoshones was none other than Sacajawea's brother! What are the odds of that?

No doubt because of reuniting long-lost Sacajawea with her brother, the Shoshone loaned Lewis and Clark horses and guided them through the mountain pass. Crossing over the mountains in the middle of August, Clark wrote in his journal, "I have been wet and as cold in every part as I ever was in my life, indeed I was at one time fearfull my feet would freeze in the thin mockersons which I wore." They came close to dying.

The Nez Perce Indians on the other side of the mountain range proved to be friendly as well, and they held onto the horses while the party headed west in several canoes. Rushing against the cold of winter, they took the Clearwater River to the Snake River, hitting the mighty Columbia River in the middle of October.

A month later, they finally made it to the Pacific Ocean!

But now they were stuck. It was winter, it was wet (which is normal for the Washington/Oregon coast), and it was miserably cold.

They all voted, even York and Sacajawea, and decided to stay put rather than try to return in the dead of winter. By present-day Astoria, Oregon, they built another fort. They named it Fort Clatsop, after the local Clatsop Indians.

66 Who put their foot in the Missouri River first: Lewis or Clark? Who cares! 99

- BUZZ ALDRIN, THE SECOND MAN ON THE MOON

It was a horrible, wet, soggy, cold winter, but they all survived. They also continued with their map making, journaling, sample taking, talking with local Indians, and more. Clark's maps, which he was always working on, would be printed upon their return, and used for the next 40 years until other explorers added to his maps and thereby created even better ones.

Incidentally, today if you drove from St. Louis, Missouri, to Astoria, Oregon, the shortest route by car is over 2,000 miles and would take you more than 30 hours to drive it. The route Lewis and Clark took was almost 4,000 miles and took them a year and a half.

The Lewis and Clark Expedition Ends

Near the end of March 1806, they began to reverse their journey. It would take them six months.

The Nez Perce Indians still had their horses, but the pass back through the mountains was snowed in. They had to wait for several weeks for the snow to melt. Finally, in early July, they crossed the mountains.

Instead of following the exact same route the whole way back to St. Louis, Lewis went north to scout out the other river that fed into the Missouri (called Marias River today). And Clark went south with Sacajawea back through Shoshone territory and then across the southern part of today's Montana.

They met back up where the Missouri River had split, which was not all that far from Fort Mandan. Lewis and his crew had run into some Blackfeet Indians and a fight ensued. Two Indians were killed in the fight, but Lewis and his men were able to escape unscathed and safely made it back to their rendezvous point.

When they reached Fort Mandan, they found it had been burned to the ground. Maybe it was lightning, forest fire, or local Indians. Nobody knew why. Today, there is a replica of Fort Mandan that you can visit. But the real fort was not only burned, the Missouri River changed course over time and now completely covers the area where the fort once stood.

Here, Sacajawea, her husband, and her son chose to stay. The Hidatsa Indians lived there and they were part of that tribe.

From there, it was about a six-week push by canoe back down the Missouri River to reach St. Louis. They arrived to much fanfare on September 23, 1806.

The expedition was a success. In addition to the documents, writings, maps, samples, trade relations, and knowledge they returned with, it truly did open the West to the general American population.

St. Louis had been known as the "Gateway to the West" because it was the last stopping point before going into uncharted territory. That is what today's Gateway Arch in St. Louis is all about. Built from 1963 to 1965, the 630-foot-tall arch is also called the Jefferson National Expansion Memorial.

Jefferson's plan worked, thanks to the capable Lewis and Clark, their crew, Sacajawea, friendly Indians, and a whole lot of good luck.

Life After the Lewis and Clark Expedition

Apparently, everyone on the expedition (except York) received a government land grant as a "thank you" for all their efforts. Lewis and Clark received the most (1,600 acres each and extra pay), as well as titles with positions. Lewis was appointed the next year to be governor of the Upper Louisiana Territory and Clark was appointed Brigadier General of the militia for the Upper Louisiana Territory.

Clark was also appointed Indian Agent for the territory. I'm guessing that was because he was a good communicator and genuinely cared for the Indians. He seemed to have a special place in his heart for Sacajawea's family. He was able to get an interpreter job for Toussaint, who had already received money and land for his part in the expedition.

In 1809, Sacajawea, Toussaint, and four-year-old Jean Baptiste traveled down to St. Louis. Clark had invited them, but he had also offered to pay for Jean Baptiste's education. When Sacajawea and Toussaint left, they left Jean Baptiste with Clark.

That worked well because Clark had gotten married the year before to Julia Hancock. Their firstborn was a son named Meriwether Lewis, in obvious honor of his friend. Young Meriwether Lewis Clark and Jean Baptiste would grow up together, both eventually fighting in the Mexican American War.

Incidentally, Meriwether Lewis Clark would go on to have a son by the same name who would build Churchill Downs, site of the famous Kentucky Derby.

> 66 It is but justice to say that Messrs. Lewis and Clarke and their brave companions have by this arduous service deserved well of their country. 99
>
> – THOMAS JEFFERSON

As for Lewis, he had his own struggles, which included alcohol, debt, and depression. Apparently, he was also suicidal. Sadly, while traveling to Washington, D.C., in 1809 to address some issues related to his governorship, he was found dead in a cabin beside the Natchez Trace Trail. It appeared that he had shot himself, though some argue he was shot by robbers.

We will never know exactly what happened to Lewis, but it was a very sad end to someone who played such a larger-than-life role in the western expansion of the United States. His burial site and memorial are there by the Natchez Trace.

Sacajawea would also not live that long. Soon after her second child, Lizette, was born, she died in 1812 at Fort Manuel, situated on the Missouri River in South Dakota. Like Fort Mandan, Fort Manuel is now gone and under water. Sacajawea was only 24 when she died.

Interestingly, because Toussaint had so many wives during his lifetime, there was some confusion (and possible folklore) as to whether it really was Sacajawea who died in 1812 or whether it was another one of Toussaint's wives. That is why you will find Sacajawea's grave in a Shoshone graveyard in western Wyoming.

As promised, Clark adopted Jean Baptiste and Lizette and provided for their education. He added them to his growing family. He and Julia would have five children together.

Julia died unexpectedly in 1820. Clark remarried, this time to Harriet Radford, a widow with three children of her own. They would have two more. Sadly, Harriet also died (in 1831). She was buried in St. Louis in the Clark cemetery.

During this time, Clark was incredibly busy. He was always working on his memoirs and the story of the great expedition, but Clark couldn't spell his way out of a wet paper bag. He found an editor/writer to help him finish the story, which finally came out in 1814.

Clark played a part in the War of 1812, which finally expelled the British from our shores. He was appointed Governor of the Missouri Territory by President James Madison, after Thomas Jefferson's two terms in office.

Then in 1822, President James Monroe appointed him to be the Superintendent of Indian Affairs. Clark was the go-to guy for every Indian trade agreement, discussion, peace treaty, settlement, or expansion plan that included the Indians west of the Mississippi. That was a LOT of territory!

It was in this role of Superintendent of Indian Affairs that Clark probably made the biggest impact. Some people mocked him for being too friendly with the Indians, but he was still the man in the middle. It was his job to coordinate trade and manage peace.

If that's not a thankless job, I don't know what is. How do you make anyone happy when it's not always a win-win situation?

Clark was appointed and reappointed by Presidents Thomas Jefferson, James Madison, James Monroe, John Quincy Adams, Henry Clay, and Martin Van Buren. Not many people can say they've done that!

In 1838, almost 32 years exactly after the triumphant return of the Louis and Clark Expedition, William Clark died in St. Louis. He was 68 years old and buried in the Clark family cemetery there in St. Louis.

If I could ask them questions, it would be:

1. Lewis: You did the impossible with that expedition. I recognize that not much in life will compare, but don't give up on living. Why not run for president? The US needs leaders who believe in our country, take risks, and know how to work hard.

2. Clark: What's your secret to levelheadedness? You did the impossible trip, became famous, helped people with your work, experienced the loss of both of your wives and at least one child, and yet you kept going and going? How do you do it?

3. Sacajawea: If you knew in the future that you would be super famous, how would you live your life today? What choices would you make about your life and children?

All three of these explorers would have their names engraved into our nation's history books. There are so many lakes, rivers, mountain peaks, parks, and plants named after Lewis, Clark, and Sacajawea that it is hard to count them all. They even made it to the US currency and postage stamps.

Thomas Jefferson was so right! Exploring the land from his Louisiana Purchase all the way to the Pacific Ocean would indeed help open up the country.

Jefferson used to say, "One man with courage is a majority." I personally love that quote and try to live by it every single day. Our nation has always benefited when people do just that.

William Clark		Noah Webster
1770–1838		1758–1843

William Clark probably missed Noah Webster's 1783 "blue-back speller" because Clark's spelling was atrocious, but *Webster's Dictionary* from 1828 had a nod to Clark by defining "expedition" as: "Any enterprize, undertaking or attempt by a number of persons; or the collective body which undertakes. We say, **our government sent an expedition to the Pacific**; the *expedition* has arrived."

CHAPTER 8

Noah Webster

1758–1843

Back in the old days, before computers and smart phones with their "spell check" features, if you didn't know how to spell a word, you had to look it up. Oh, the horror! And usually it was in one of those big, thick hardback books on the shelf that was covered in dust.

Behold . . . the dictionary!

I don't know about you, but when I was a kid, the dictionary definitely fell in the "necessary evil" category. (My apologies if you were one of the few who actually read a dictionary for pleasure.)

Every K–12 classroom has one. Probably every home has one or two. They are everywhere and they are avoided, but they are necessary. Thankfully, we have technology today, and that has really helped with the speed in which we learn and in our ability to spell correctly.

But every book, even a dictionary, has an author. And it takes a very special type of person to write a dictionary.

The Road to the American Dictionary

In 1774, just before the Declaration of Independence and the American Revolution, 16-year-old Noah Webster went off to Yale College. His dad mortgaged the family farm in West Hartford, Connecticut, so Noah could attend. How's that for extra pressure to finish?

You may remember during the American Revolution when George Washington was fighting in New York, he asked for a volunteer to cross the river and spy on the British, and a young man by the name of Nathan Hale volunteered. Hale was recognized, captured, and hung. Standing below his gallows, Hale uttered some of the best, motivational, get-back-up-and-keep-fighting words I have ever heard. He said:

"I only regret that I have but one life to lose for my country."

Hale was a graduate of Yale College, class of 1773. Webster was already a patriot, but I'm guessing Hale's words from a fellow classmate burned in Webster's heart for the rest of his life.

Webster graduated from Yale in 1778, then taught school while studying law, passing the bar in 1781. As the American Revolution was winding down, Webster was busy teaching school.

> 66 The freedom of the press is a valuable privilege, but the abuse of it in this country is a frightful evil. 99
>
> – NOAH WEBSTER

The more he taught, the more upset he became. It was not the students or the teaching that bothered him, even though schools back then were typically crammed with many kids of varying ages in one big room. Rather, what made him mad was the fact that they used British textbooks!

There he was, a red-blooded patriot who wanted independence, teaching proper British English to children whose fathers fought to be free of England's tyranny. It didn't make any sense!

Instead of simply complaining about it, he promptly acted. In 1783, the same year that the Treaty of Paris was signed that ended the Revolutionary War, *The American Spelling Book* came off the press. It had a blue cover and became known across the country as the "blue-backed speller." It would sell millions of copies!

In his own way, deep in the bowels and vowels of the English language, Webster was at war with England. Consider his words:

"As an independent nation, our honor requires us to have a system of our own, in language as well as government. Great Britain, whose children we are, and whose language we speak, should no longer be our standard; for the taste of her writers is already corrupted, and her language on the decline."

See how he slipped with "in language as well as government" bit? He was not only telling the British off, but he was showing the logic behind his changes to the language.

But really, how revolutionary is a spelling book?

Think about it for a second. If your language is not the same, if the spelling is not the same, and if the accent is not the same, then you are not the same. And if you are not the same, why are you willing to be controlled?

It's hard to argue with that!

Now, language naturally changes and evolves over time (as Webster very well knew and taught), but there is also a time when you get to choose one version over another. And Webster was choosing!

His "blue-backed speller" was *American* English. We Americans had been here for 200 years at that point. That's nothing compared to the English in England, but there was already some variation in the language. Webster took that into account, but he also pushed for greater change and clear differences.

A few obvious examples of his changes from British English to American English include:

- honour – honor
- labour – labor
- colour – color

And some of my favorite changes:
- centre – center
- theatre – theater
- fibre – fiber

Within a single generation, the differences in the language were set in stone. Virtually every school-age child used his speller. As a direct result, people were speaking, spelling, and writing in American English.

Oh, if you hated spelling bees growing up, you can blame Noah Webster for that. It was his "blue-backed speller" that gave rise to local spelling competitions. Over time, these grew to be national and then international.

> " A national language is a band of national union. "
>
> – Noah Webster

Though his spelling book was a best seller, Webster didn't stop there. That was just the beginning! His crowning achievement was yet to come. It was a dream that would take him almost 30 years to complete!

His masterpiece was his dictionary, eventually making his name virtually synonymous with the word "dictionary" itself. It would be the largest English dictionary in the world at that time.

To create his 70,000-word dictionary, of which almost 15 percent were words that had never been in a dictionary before, Webster became a one-man linguistic machine.

- He traveled the country (as much as he could in the early 1800s) taking notes on how Americans spoke.
- He learned and studied more than 25 languages so he could use them in his dictionary.
- He spent many months in England and France, writing and doing research.
- He studied everything in every known field so he could include it.

He also did something else that I especially love. He purposefully wove America, her morals, the Bible, freedom, American history, independence, and more into his textbooks. For example, his definition of "retire" includes this:

To withdraw from a public station. General Washington, in 1796, retired to private life.

Not only did some people call Webster the Schoolmaster of the Nation, but some also called him the Forgotten Founding Father. No wonder! He fought in his own way for America's freedom. He knew that linguistics would eventually lead to politics.

In 1828, his two-volume *An American Dictionary of the English Language* was published. Webster would be forever immortalized for this accomplishment.

But Webster, age 70, was not about to retire.

The Life of Noah Webster

Webster's hometown of West Hartford, Connecticut, is only about 115 miles west of Plymouth, Massachusetts, where the Pilgrims landed in 1620. His mother was a direct descendant of William Bradford, the governor who also wrote a book about the Pilgrims and their rough beginnings in Plymouth.

Maybe writing was in his genes, for Webster would go on to become one of America's most prolific writers of all time.

The success of Webster's "blue-back speller" from 1783 helped enable him years later to focus on creating his dictionary. Even then, it was still a financial stretch.

Webster married Rebecca Greenleaf in 1789, and they had eight children together. As was so common back then, one of them, died in infancy.

They moved briefly to New York City so Webster could edit the *Federalist Party* newspaper. While there, he started two newspapers, which he sold a few years later.

In 1798, they returned to New Haven, Connecticut. Soon after, he was elected to Connecticut's House of Representatives. It was here that he began work on his dictionary.

During the years in New Haven, the presidency turned from President Adams to President Jefferson, and then came the great Louisiana Purchase in 1803 and the Great Expedition in 1804 to 1806. Involved in politics, well-traveled, and a voracious researcher, Webster no doubt tracked the journey of Lewis and Clark. In his 1828 dictionary, the word "expedition" contains a direct nod to the great expedition.

At age 50, something happened that would forever change his life. It was 1808 and his two eldest daughters invited him and Rebecca to a revival meeting. They went and were touched by God. He had grown up in a Christian home, but this was different. He was changed. He was born again.

Deeply impacted, he continued with his work. Now, more than ever, he wove the Bible into everything he did. His dictionary would have more Bible in it (more than 6,000 Bible references) than any other reference book in his day.

Years later, he wrote:

"The Bible is the chief moral cause of all that is *good*, and the best corrector of all that is *evil,* in human society; the *best* book for regulating the temporal concerns of men, and the *only book* that can serve as an infallible guide to the future felicity."

I think he was using his platform, creating a dictionary that the entire nation would use, to point readers to the God who was referenced everywhere by our Founding Fathers, to remember why the nation says "In God we trust," and to keep our standards and morals high.

66 To travel far, there is no better ship than a book. 99

– EMILY DICKINSON

Absolutely nothing wrong with that!

In 1812, when their youngest child was four years old, they moved 90 miles north to Amherst, Massachusetts. During the 10 years that they lived there, Webster helped found Amherst College with Samuel Dickinson, who was a lawyer, church deacon, town clerk, and state representative.

This Samuel Dickinson would be the grandfather of Emily Dickinson, who would be born in Amherst in 1830 and later attend Amherst College. Interestingly, Emily was known to be one of Webster's most avid readers.

All the while, Webster continued working on his dictionary. His nearly 30-year undertaking would have been impossible for most people, but Webster had the ability to stay focused, and bit by bit, complete his massive two-volume dictionary. He would be the last lexicographer to single-handedly create a dictionary.

They returned to New Haven, Connecticut, in 1822. Two years later, his dictionary almost complete, Webster traveled to Europe and spent many months in England and France doing further research for his dictionary.

I can't even imagine the level of complexity and organization that goes into choosing, defining, historically researching, and correctly pronouncing a single word, let alone 70,000 words!

That's mind-blowing. And this was back when everything was manual. They didn't even have typewriters. Those would come 40 years later.

Finally, in 1828, his dictionary was finished . . . but he wasn't! He immediately launched into a battle for copyright protection. Why the need? Because America was a new country and didn't have very good copyright protection laws in place.

Remember the millions and millions of copies of his "blue-back speller"? Well, most of those were pirated.

Thanks to Webster's dictionary, his urging, speaking to the House of Representatives, and talking with President Andrew Jackson, the Copyright Act of 1831 was signed into law.

It doubled copyright protection from 14 to 28 years, with an option to renew for 14 more years. This would positively impact every writer, musician, publisher, and printer across the nation.

Now 73 years old, Webster still wasn't done.

He started working on his own version of the Bible! Using the 1611 version of the King James Bible, he made minor changes in the area of grammar, outdated words, and words he felt were offensive to readers at that time. All in all, he didn't change much.

What he wanted to do was increase the readership of the Bible by making it easier to read. He didn't have an ax to grind and had no intention of creating drama. He simply wanted more people to read the Bible.

He wrote:

"I have attempted to render the English version more useful, by correcting a few obvious errors, and removing some obscurities, with objectionable words and phrases; and my earnest prayer is, that my labors may not be wholly unsuccessful."

Even though his effort was the biggest undertaking since the King James version came out over 220 years earlier, people still loved the old King James Version. They put up with the archaic words and odd spelling.

In short, Webster's Bible of 1833 was pretty much a dud.

Interestingly, his Bible is public domain, and you can download it for free (archive.org/details/The-Webster-Bible).

66 Education is useless without the Bible. 99

– Noah Webster

Webster then wrote a book to defend the Bible and Christianity as a whole. It was called *Value of the Bible and Excellence of the Christian Religion* and was published the year after his Bible.

His famous 1828 dictionary sold out of its first printing, but it wasn't a bestseller like his "blue-back speller."

The very nature of a dictionary is that it must be constantly tweaked, updated, added to, revised, changed, and reprinted. Due to less than expected sales, and with the need for his second edition, Webster mortgaged his home. His father had done the same for Webster more than 60 years earlier.

Unfortunately for Webster, his debts would plague him for the rest of his life.

In 1840, the second edition of his dictionary was published.

Webster being Webster, he kept tinkering, tweaking, and updating his dictionary until his death in 1843. He couldn't help himself. I personally don't think he knew how to take a break, but always working certainly kept him young and active.

Just before his death, surrounded by family and his pastor, 85-year-old Webster expressed his trust in God and his gratefulness for the life he had.

If I could have somehow been allowed in to ask him a few questions, there would have been no time or need to talk about trivialities. In truth, almost everything is trivial when you are on your deathbed! I would still have wanted to ask:

1. Is there more that you wish you had said or done?
2. What can we do today to carry your vision forward?
3. What warnings do you see for us as a nation?
4. How can we stay focused on what's most important?
5. What would you tell the future generation if you could talk with them now?
6. Can you tell me about this peace you have with God?

Webster was buried in Grove Street Cemetery, which today is basically in the middle of the Yale campus in New Haven, Connecticut.

His wife, Rebecca, would be buried beside him four short years later.

The Merriam-Webster Dictionary

What happened to Webster's dictionary? It was just too good to pass into obscurity. What's more, Webster's name was the known brand for all things dictionary related.

Two brothers, George and Charles Merriam, understood that fact and quickly stepped in and purchased the rights to Webster's second edition. I'm sure that pleased Rebecca and the family.

The Merriam brothers ran a print shop and bookstore in Springfield, Massachusetts, which is on the route between New Haven and Amherst. That means Webster would have traveled through Springfield repeatedly when he went back and forth between the towns.

In 1847, the same year Rebecca died, they published a revised version of Webster's dictionary. And countless editions later, we have the world-famous *Merriam-Webster Dictionary*.

Webster's dictionary would be a perpetual profit center. He just didn't get to enjoy that fact.

Ironically, just as it was back in Webster's day, I think every classroom and every home today has one of his dictionaries. Even with all the changes and updates, Webster's name lives on.

Noah Webster **Eli Whitney**
1758–1843 1765–1825

Both Noah Webster and Eli Whitney went to Yale (classes of 1778 and 1792, respectively), lived in New Haven, Connecticut, at the same time, and would both be buried in the Grove Street Cemetery in New Haven. Webster included Whitney in his 1828 dictionary.

CHAPTER 9

Eli Whitney

1765–1825

Some inventions are random bursts of inspiration, while others are more the result of a known need that up to that point has gone unmet, unanswered, and unfulfilled.

Eli Whitney, who famously created the cotton gin, is one of the latter. He saw an obvious need and figured out how to meet that need. His invention in turn brought massive financial benefits to the entire country and then the whole world.

A cotton gin, as Noah Webster described it in his 1828 dictionary, is:

"A machine to separate the seeds from cotton, invented by that celebrated mechanician, E. Whitney."

Whitney was quite the little mechanic and entrepreneur, even from a young age. Not only could he take apart his dad's watch, but he could actually put it back together! I give him 10 points for that.

By age 14, Whitney was running his own little business from one of their farm buildings. He had created his own nail press contraption and was cranking out the nails and selling them.

It was a taste of what was to come.

Born into a farming family in 1765, Whitney's home in Westborough, Massachusetts, was a mere 60 miles from Plymouth and 30 miles west of Boston. He was too young to participate in the American Revolution, but like many in his part of the country, he wanted to attend nearby Yale College.

Unfortunately for Whitney, his stepmother (his birth mother died when he was young) wasn't too keen on the idea. That meant if he was going to attend, he would have to pay his own way.

Eventually, after working where he could, he saved up enough money to pay for college. He graduated from Yale in 1792. His focus was on science and industry.

And like many others at the time, including Noah Webster (who did become a lawyer), Whitney thought of practicing law, but there was very little business for lawyers so soon after the American Revolution. Instead of studying law, he went back to tutoring.

The now 27-year-old Whitney found work as a private tutor in South Carolina and boarded a ship for the long ride south.

It was here, on board the ship, that Whitney's future changed course. It would be another one of those "providential happenings" that just so happened to help shape our nation. Much like Squanto (helping the Pilgrims) and Sacajawea (helping Lewis and Clark) being in the right place at the right time, so would Whitney meet someone who "just so happened" to be a passenger on the same ship.

The person he met was Catherine Greene, a very savvy widow from Georgia who offered him a tutoring job at her Mulberry Grove plantation on the Savannah River just north of Savannah, Georgia.

Who Was Catherine Greene?

Catherine Greene had married, in 1774, Nathanael Greene, who would go on to be a major general in George Washington's Continental Army.

> 66 I am determined to defend my rights and maintain my freedom or sell my life in the attempt. 99

> – Nathanael Greene

She was sharp, observant, a quick decision maker, and a good judge of people. Why? Because she had been through the school of hard knocks and graduated with a PhD!

Growing up in Rhode Island, many of her family members were involved in government, so she knew how politics worked. Formally educated, she was already a step above.

During the Revolution, instead of staying at their home in Rhode Island, she joined Nathanael wherever he was stationed. Washington had put the very capable Nathanael Greene in charge of the southern states. As a military wife and mother (they had five children together), she learned to juggle all the working parts.

But when the war was over in 1783, her world fell apart.

She knew the army under Nathanael's command had been repeatedly short on supplies. She most likely knew that Nathanael had personally paid for some of the supplies. She may have also known that he had at times put his name on the line as a guarantor for necessary supplies.

But she had no idea that some of the suppliers were not honest and that they would back out of their promises, which left Nathanael holding the tab.

They were suddenly in debt and could not pay.

Nathanael had been granted land in Georgia for his war efforts. It was the abandoned 2,000-acre Mulberry Grove planation on the Savannah River, and Nathanael packed up the family and moved there in 1785. He had decided he would be a rice farmer and rebuild their fortunes.

The Georgia heat was too much for Nathanael. He died of a sunstroke the next year. He was only 43 years old.

A widow at age 31 and with many children in tow, Greene knew it was make or break time. She hired Phineas Miller, the children's tutor, to manage the plantation, and within a few short years, the plantation was humming along.

Then she appealed to Congress through her network of political friends, asking for help with the debt Nathanael had run up to help the country win the war. In 1792, George Washington himself, who was president at the time, approved her request. The cloud of debt was finally swept away.

That was the year she met Whitney on the ship bound for South Carolina. She knew talent when she saw it. If his tutoring deal didn't work out, he was welcome at Mulberry Grove.

In 1796, Greene would marry her plantation manager, Phineas Miller, who had helped her turn it into a success. Who should attend their wedding in Philadelphia? None other than George and Martha Washington.

Inventing the Cotton Gin (Cotton Engine)

Apparently, Whitney soon found out that his tutoring job paid less than he was promised. He promptly took Catherine Greene up on her offer . . . and stepped into his destiny.

Soon after arriving at Mulberry Grove, Whitney met Phineas Miller. Whitney and Miller quickly became friends as both knew farming, were entrepreneurial and business minded, and were fellow graduates of Yale.

While at Mulberry Grove, Whitney was brought up to speed on the crops, soil, farming, sales, trends, and geography. Someone, probably Miller, explained that the best type of cotton to grow in the interior of the cotton-growing states had seeds that were very difficult to pull out. The cotton extraction process was so slow and so manual that producing that type of cotton was not worth the time or money.

To add even more pressure to the situation, England had recently mechanized the process of spinning, which basically meant the making of thread or yarn from bales of wool or cotton was fast, efficient, and cheap.

In short, the market in all of Europe was ready. Everything was in place. They just needed more cotton. But without a way for cotton growers to quickly clean the cotton, they had nothing to take to market.

Talk about a need that was begging to be met!

The southern states were basically stuck. The cotton with seeds that easily came out could only be grown on the coast, and they had maxed that out already. The market for tobacco was shrinking as well. Without an answer, the entire economy of the south was basically in pause mode.

Whitney's brain immediately went to work. If he could help one plantation, then he could help an entire state. And whoever found the answer would be rich!

Within a few months, he created a crude model that could separate the cotton from the seeds. Catherine Greene provided the necessary financial backing.

After more tweaks and refinements, and after Whitney and Miller formed a company and filed a US patent (officially approved in 1794), the cotton gin was ready. It could do an entire day's work in a single hour.

What farmer in any southern state wouldn't benefit from that? The massive growth potential was obvious.

As soon as farmers heard about it, they immediately started planting more cotton. Every farmer could join in. Being on or near the coast was no longer an issue.

> 66 I never thought my cotton gin would change history. 99
>
> – ELI WHITNEY

The business model that Whitney and Miller came up with was to provide the farmers with the cotton gins in exchange for 40 percent of the crop's value. Basically, they would be the middlemen, processing the cotton for a slice of the profits.

It was a good idea on paper, but the cotton gin had ignited a firestorm that could not be contained. It was far bigger than they imagined. You could call it the perfect storm.

Four things happened simultaneously that completely blew them out of the water.

First, farmers were not too excited about a middleman. Sure, their crops would be huge in comparison to what they had been before, but still, they didn't want to "lose" 40 percent of anything.

Second, the demand for their cotton gins was greater than they were able to produce in time to meet the limitless demand. The market was simply too big and too hungry.

Third, the mechanics of the cotton gin was so simple that other people took the cotton gin apart and built their own. They immediately started producing their own copycat versions, which the farmers immediately purchased.

Fourth, neither the government nor the states enforced the US patent that Whitney had received. So much for copyright protection!

Naturally, Whitney and Miller fought back. They were in the right, after all! They had a patent, it was their company that first produced the cotton gins, and everyone knew it. Surely their lawyers could take their case to court and win, right? Not in the slightest.

Sadly, the states seemed to pretend they didn't notice. Cotton was king, and everyone rushed to cash in on it.

Whitney and Miller spent their profits on lawyers and were bankrupt and out of business just five years later! To add insult to injury, when it came time to renew the cotton gin patent, the government refused! No wonder Whitney is quoted as saying, "An invention can be so valuable as to be worthless to the inventor."

Though neither Whitney nor Miller got wealthy with the cotton gin, the southern states sure did. Cotton soon became the nation's greatest export and would hold that number one position for decades!

Naturally, the cotton gin increased the need for more farm laborers. The more cotton a farmer could plant, the more money he would make. Demand was high and the cotton gin made it possible to make an immediate profit.

That meant the farmers with the most slaves had the greatest money-making potential. They could simply plant and harvest more cotton. Sadly, the slave trade increased as a result.

The money-making cycle in the southern states seemed to have no end.

Imagine making something so good that everyone wanted it—but you got nothing for it. Talk about demoralizing! I'm not sure how I would have reacted after that massive letdown.

But not Whitney. He bounced right back. You simply can't keep a good man down.

The Next Big Thing – Interchangeable Parts

Prior to the 1801 purchase of the Louisiana Territory, the US and France were at odds. War seemed to be a possibility. Thankfully, war was avoided.

The US government had a problem they could not seem to be able to fix. It was a problem that plagued every person, city, and state, but it was the government that felt it the most.

What was the problem? The lack of guns. Specifically, the production of a gun was too slow. If war came, they were in trouble.

You see, up until this point in history, every gun was made by hand. Each part, each piece, was hand crafted by a gunsmith. And if a part broke, the repair process was also a very tedious, manual process.

Once again, there was a massive need. Could Whitney come up with an answer?

He believed he could. He entered his bid into the pot, along with other firms that hoped to win the government contract for 10,000 guns, and he won!

His bid also had a due date: just two years! That meant creating one new gun every 30 minutes per eight-hour day, seven days a week, for two straight years!

The only way it would be remotely possible was if the guns were built from interchangeable parts. Basically, if each part of a gun was mass produced, then a gun could be assembled from those parts. This would exponentially speed up the production process and virtually eliminate any time it took to repair a gun.

Whitney was not the first person to think of interchangeable parts, nor was he the only person to see the value of such parts, but he was the first person to build a gun factory based on the interchangeable parts concept.

Whitney moved back to Connecticut and, just 3.5 miles north of New Haven, Connecticut, on Mill River, he created a factory. It was the Whitney Armory, established in 1798.

This is where his creative juices really flowed! Around his factory, he built houses and let his workers live there for free. He even had a school for the workers' children. Great incentive to stick around!

His own little town was called Whitneyville, which still exists today. The armory is now the Eli Whitney Museum.

> 66 One of my primary objects is to form the tools so the tools themselves shall fashion the work and give to every part its just proportion. 99
>
> – ELI WHITNEY

Two years later, Whitney had not produced a single gun. What he had done was create the machinery and systems necessary to create all the parts for the guns. It took him 10 years to fulfill his order of 10,000 guns.

When an order for 15,000 guns came in, he fulfilled it in two years! His interchangeable parts system worked. The machine age was born!

Once again, Whitney had come up with an invention that not only benefited the country, it benefited the world.

His armory would continue to prosper, eventually being run by his son, Eli Whitney Jr.

Pausing for Family

You could safely say that Whitney was a workaholic. He went from working as a teen, working to get to college, working on his cotton gin, and then working at his armory to fulfill all the contracts he had.

It was a good life, but he had never really paused to think of a family. His cotton gin business partner, Phineas Miller, had married Catherine Greene, but sadly, Miller died in 1803 and Greene in 1814.

All this while, Whitney worked his tail off. He had never married, but he eventually grew tired of being a bachelor.

Finally, in 1817, he married Henrietta Edwards. She was the granddaughter of Jonathan Edwards, the preacher who played a part in America's First Great Awakening.

They had four children together, three girls and a boy. The son they named Eli Whitney Jr. But since Whitney's father was also named Eli, all three generations had the same name. Whitney's father would be Sr., he was just Whitney, and his son was Jr.

Incredibly, his life would come to an end only eight years later. He died after a short battle with prostate cancer. He was only 59 years old. His death, according to his obituary, was a "public calamity" for the nation.

Truly it was.

Though Whitney had not benefited as much from his inventions as he hoped, you could say that he sowed good seed, because his son, Eli Whitney Jr., would pick up where he left off.

Whitney was buried in Grove Street Cemetery in New Haven, Connecticut, sharing it with many greats, including Noah Webster, who though older, would die 18 years later.

If I could somehow get a few minutes with Whitney, I would really like to know just one thing:

> No doubt you thought about this a million times, but what could you have done differently with your cotton gin so that you actually made a profit? What business model could have handled the rapid growth to your benefit?

Seriously, that is THE question of all time!

To have created something so big, so profitable, so insanely simple, and walk away with nothing to show for it. That boggles my mind.

I think Whitney would have been one of the richest people in all of history had he been able to capture a portion of the profits from his cotton gin invention.

But the fact that Whitney could overcome that loss, keep inventing, and succeed all over again is a testament to his attitude and perseverance. I want to be like that when I grow up.

Eli Whitney
1765–1825

Samuel Colt
1814–1862

Samuel Colt fulfilled his most important order of 1,000 Walker Colts in the very armory that Eli Whitney built. That event helped boost both Colt's business as well as that of Eli Whitney Jr. Both Colt and Whitney sent a son to Yale.

CHAPTER 10

Samuel Colt

1814–1862

Many of the household names you see around the world today cut their teeth in the business of war, such as Volkswagen, Mitsubishi, and Colt.

Here in America, almost everyone has heard of Colt, as in the revolver that helped tame the Wild West. And if we don't see them as much anymore, you'll find them in western movies. Several of Clint Eastwood's westerns were with a Colt.

As with many inventions, the need comes first and then the answers follow. That was the way it worked for Eli Whitney, and that was the way it worked for Samuel Colt.

Incidentally, Colt not only built upon the interchangeable parts approach that Eli Whitney took to mass producing guns, but he also built revolvers out of Whitney's own armory when he worked with Eli Whitney Jr.

The Man Behind the Legend

Born in 1814 in Hartford, Connecticut, Colt grew up only 35 miles north of Whitneyville, Connecticut, where Whitney was busy building guns.

My guess is that Colt not only knew of Whitney's gun armory, but he heard of how Whitney treated his employees, for Colt would do something similar years later with his employees when he had his own gun factory.

Young Colt was the ultimate pyromaniac. He learned (probably by trial and error!) how to make gunpowder, fireworks, and underwater explosives. What's more, he knew how to use electricity to set it off!

At age 15, the family lived in Ware, Massachusetts, which is 70 miles straight west of Boston. He worked in his father's textile business, which exposed Colt to machines, tools, mass production, parts, and the need for more customers.

During that time, Colt had the idea of putting an explosive-laden raft out on a pond and, on July 4th, he would detonate it with his own specially made fuse wire (tarred rope with a wire running through it).

Being a natural promoter and showman, he printed up a flyer and circulated it around town, teasing people with these words:

"Sam'l colt will blow a raft skyhigh on Ware pond, July 4. 1829."

People came from far and wide to gather around the pond. Who wouldn't? Blowing things up is always an attraction.

The raft did explode, though maybe not "skyhigh" enough for some people. The only drawback was that a lot of people dressed in their Sunday best got splattered with pond scum and mud. If you've ever had stinky pond sludge on you or your clothes, you know how bad it smells and how hard it is to get it out of your clothes. And if you were wearing white, good luck!

His muddy escapade did net him one gain. He met a machinist who was a few years older than him. This machinist, Elisha K. Root, would end up working in Colt's gun factory 20 years later, helping improve the guns and the machines that forged the parts. Root would even become the president of Colt's company when Colt died.

The next July 4th would spell trouble for Colt. He and two friends decided that shooting off an old American Revolution cannon (that was on display outside Amherst Academy) nice and early July 4th morning would be a good idea. This is the same school that Noah Webster and Emily Dickinson's grandfather helped to found. Emily would attend 10 years after Colt did.

But Colt would not graduate from Amherst Academy. As you might imagine, the powers that be were not impressed with Colt's antics or the cannon blasting everyone awake. He was promptly expelled. The school had put up with his explosions throughout the year, and his little July 4th escapade was the final straw.

Colt went to sea after that, most likely at the recommendation of his father. After all, getting out of town, out of the news, and away from troublemakers would be good. However, I'm not sure how that logic works for the troublemaker himself.

Life as a seaman on a ship is pretty regimented. There are duties to perform, hours at the helm, hours on watch, loading and unloading, cargo to stow, chain from the anchor to manhandle in place, lines to prepare, decks to scrub, and so much more, all while trying not to get seasick and to avoid storms. It's a hard life, and perhaps that was the plan for young Colt.

While at sea, en route to Calcutta (Kolkata today), India, a voyage that would take four to six months, Colt no doubt spent hours behind the wheel or on duty near the wheel. The ship's steering wheel controlled the ship's rudder and was usually held in place by the person who was on duty at the helm. The officer called out the heading and the seaman turned and held the wheel accordingly. The wheel could also be latched or lashed in place if the seas were calm.

The wheel fascinated Colt. In his mind, he saw the wheel as a cylinder of a gun, with holes where bullets went, and a gun that could fire repeatedly as the cylinder spun from bullet to bullet, firing at least five times before reloading.

While at sea, he carved himself a working model. It didn't fire bullets, of course, but it showed the concept of a spinning cylinder that could turn and click into place, ready to fire each time the trigger was pulled.

Single-shot muskets were the norm, but their single-shot capability proved dangerous if you were being attacked by an enemy, a wild animal, or an American Indian. Being able to fire multiple shots without stopping to reload would be a game changer!

Colt knew that, which was why his entrepreneurial and inventive mind was spinning faster than the cylinder of his gun.

The Colt Firearm Is Born

When he returned, he took his wood model to a local gunsmith. Together, they created an actual working pistol and rifle with a multi-shot cylinder.

Then in 1832, at age 18, Colt headed down to Washington, D.C., to patent his creation, generate interest, perhaps get funding, and maybe even to get a government contract. He was well received and his guns did generate interest, but he was advised to further perfect his creation before filing a patent. His patent is dated 1836, proof that he listened to the advice.

Perfecting the gun meant making a lot more guns in the process, and Colt simply didn't have that kind of money. Most 18-year-olds are a little cash strapped, so Colt had to figure out a way to generate enough money to fund his endeavor.

Being the bold, audacious showman that he was, he branded himself "Dr. Coult" who came from faraway places (including Calcutta) and went on the road with his own little freak show. More of an oddity show, really, for he charged people 25 cents to come to his show, hear him speak, inhale helium, talk mysteriously in a high-pitched voice for a few minutes, and laugh hilariously at each other.

> 66 The good people of this world are very far from being satisfied with each other and my arms are the best peacemakers. 99
>
> – SAMUEL COLT

It worked. He traveled up and down the coast and all across the states. He didn't go west of the Mississippi River as that wasn't very populated at that time, though the Louisiana Purchase had already happened. Americans were heading west, but he kept his show to the cities. After all, the bigger the city, the more customers he would have. In some places, he did two performances a night.

After a few years, and pouring his profits into his gun creation, he finally had two improved five-shot models, a pistol and a rifle. He applied for and received his patents.

Finally, patent in hand, he was ready for business!

Investors quickly caught the vision and put money into Colt's Patent Arms Manufacturing Company. Only 22 years old, Colt had his own armory. He set up his business in Paterson, New Jersey, which is pretty much right across the Hudson River from New York and just 80 miles down the coast from New Haven, Connecticut.

Just as Eli Whitney had done, Colt wanted to produce guns that were made from interchangeable parts. It only made sense, as did the assembly line approach to creating each gun.

The five-shot Patterson was born!

Next up, Colt needed customers. He was ready for a government contract. Why not? They needed a lot of guns and he could make a lot of guns. It seemed simple enough.

Colt traveled to Washington, D.C., and gave demonstrations, even to President Andrew Jackson. However, the president was not impressed. Perhaps the adage, "If it ain't broke, don't fix it" applies here.

He even traveled to Florida (it wasn't a state until 1845) to demonstrate his Patterson pistol directly to the soldiers fighting the Seminole Indians. Instead of talking with the slow-moving bureaucrats in Washington, he figured talking with those in the field would get him better results. The reaction was mixed, some liked it and some didn't, and he sold about half of the guns he brought, but either way, Colt did not get the big government contracts he was looking for.

Even the Battle of the Alamo, which happened earlier that year (March of 1836), was not enough incentive to better arm our soldiers.

> 66 Without your pistols we would not have had the confidence to have undertaken such daring adventures. 99
>
> – SAMUEL WALKER, TEXAS RANGER CAPTAIN

Unfortunately, Colt needed sizeable orders in order to turn a profit. Making guns for individuals to purchase was always part of the plan, and they were doing that, but his guns sold for about four times what single-shot muskets sold for. It was an uphill sale at every level.

Also, though the Patterson was much better than a single-shot pistol, it was still a little cumbersome when it came time to reload.

He was stuck. Try as he might, gun show after gun show, demonstration after demonstration, even hosting dinners with liberal amounts of alcohol, Colt was unable to land a contract for his guns. He simply didn't have enough customers.

Despite all his wheeling and dealing, he just couldn't get any government contracts. By 1840, his company was out of money. The doors of his armory closed.

Just like Eli Whitney with his cotton gin, Colt went from boom to bust in about five years.

But as with Whitney, you can't keep a good man down! Colt turned back to something else he had experience with—underwater mines.

Blowing Things Up!

Within a year, Colt was back in business. This time with mines for the navy. His mines could be placed in any body of water, and with his waterproof wire that ran from the mine all the way to land, could be detonated remotely with the flip of a switch.

This did generate enough government interest that Congress gave him $6,000 toward underwater mines. He was also able to get individual investors to join in.

During this process, he befriended Samuel F. B. Morse, who was busy working on the telegraph. They would become friends and help each other out with their respective areas of expertise. Colt helped Morse with some of his telegraph projects, such as running telegraph cables through water, but Colt's focus was on blowing things up.

He spent three years creating mines, laying wire, blowing up ships, amazing spectators, and satisfying Congress, but when all was said and done, the government again decided that it didn't want to invest money into mines for defense. They didn't see it as a true need.

Sure, if America was at war, such as she had been with England just a few decades before, it would have been an easy sale. Every port city and harbor would have been a viable place to put Colt's mines. But America was not at war.

Without a pressing need, the expense could not be justified, and Colt walked away empty-handed.

And then America found itself at war again.

The Colt Firearm Is Reborn

Remember the guns that Colt took down to Florida where he managed to sell about half of them to the soldiers fighting the Seminole Indians? Apparently, enough of the soldiers got proficient at using his five-shot guns that they became a formidable force.

And either some of those men became Texas Rangers or the guns ended up in the hands of the Texas Rangers, but in 1844, 15 Rangers fought it out with about 80 Comanche Indians in the Texas hill country, north of San Antonio and west of Austin.

The result was an incredible victory for the Rangers. Instead of firing once and having to reload, during which time the Comanches would have wiped them out, the five-shot guns gave the Rangers 75 immediate shots, which proved more than enough.

One of those Rangers was the legendary Samuel Walker. He was adept at using the Colt. He loved it, praised it, and figured he had a few ways to improve it should the opportunity ever present itself.

In less than 12 months, America would be at war with Mexico. The Mexican-American War (with William Clark's son and Sacajawea's son fighting in it) was on. It was May of 1846.

There was an instant need for more of those handy five-shot Colts. Samuel Walker went north and met with Colt, and Walker brought his list of modifications. He wanted more bang and he wanted more shots.

I don't know the size of Walker's wrists, but the "hand cannon" as it was soon called was not for the weak-kneed or faint of heart. It could stop a charging man or animal dead in its tracks. The recoil must have been something fierce, not to mention deafening. Understandably, it was the biggest caliber pistol that our military ever used.

The conversation probably went something like this:

"Can you produce a bigger caliber, six-shot gun?"

"Of course. Not a problem."

"Can you deliver 1,000 of them to us in three months?"

"Of course. Not a problem."

But it was a problem. Not only did Colt need to redesign his gun, he also had no armory. His gun factory in Paterson, New Jersey, had been closed for several years.

Not to worry! Colt moved forward with lightning speed. He finally had his big government contract for 1,000 Colt pistols and he was going to fulfill it. Walker gave Colt a second chance at success, and Colt would not miss it.

He boldly asked the best gunsmiths he knew to help by supplying him with the necessary redesigned parts. Then he went to Eli Whitney Jr. and asked for permission to assemble the 1,000 new six-shot pistols at his Whitneyville armory, the cotton gin for inventory that Eli Whitney had built almost 50 years earlier.

And they did it! Within three months, 1,000 brand-new six-shot Walker-Colt pistols were delivered. It was a stunning success.

Sadly, Texas Ranger Captain Samuel Walker was killed the following year while fighting in Huamantla, Mexico, which is 90 miles east of Mexico City. He was wearing a pair of Walker-Colts the day of his death. His body was taken to San Antonio, Texas, and buried.

Orders started pouring in!

Colt moved back to Hartford, Connecticut. It was only 35 miles north of Whitneyville where he had been working in Eli Whitney Jr.'s armory. Colt needed his own armory, so he created a factory that mirrored many of the employee-friendly aspects of his predecessor, Eli Whitney.

Eli Whitney Jr. went on to produce his own version of a pistol at his armory, becoming quite wealthy in the process. He eventually sold his armory to the Winchester gun company in 1888 and went into other successful business ventures.

Up in Hartford, Colt positioned his Patent Fire Arms Manufacturing Company on the Connecticut River. It would become his dream, the efficient blend of interchangeable parts and assembly line production. They operated on 10-hour workdays and were able to produce 15 Colts every hour!

66 A man's rights rest in three boxes: the ballot box, the jury box, and the cartridge box. 99

– FREDERICK DOUGLASS (1818-1895)

If you do the math, that's more than 50,000 guns in a year, and they were doing just that!

His old friend, Elisha Root, whom he had met 20 years earlier when he blew up the raft on Ware Pond, was his superintendent and helped create the most technologically advanced production system of its time. Root perfected many milling machines and made improvements to the guns that helped make Colt even more prosperous.

Colt kept coming up with better and better models that used less parts, weighed less, were easier to reload, shot more accurately, were more durable, and more. Models include the Dragoon, Peacemaker, 1849 Pocket, 1851 Navy, and 1860 Army, to name a few.

The boom time showed no signs of stopping.

When the Mexican-American War ended in 1848, the West was fully open. You could go from one end of the country to the other, but it was not safe. Having a six-shot Colt was definitely necessary.

Then the gold rushes in California hit. First in 1848, then in infamous 1949 (hence, the "forty-niners"), and beyond, gold was a magnet that brought tens of thousands of people to California. Many came across the newly obtained land that Mexico lost after the Mexican-American War, and they faced animals, thieves, and Indians. Having a Colt was a straight-up necessity.

Until trains could cross the entire nation, which didn't happen until 1869, westward migration via wagon, horse, or stagecoach usually required some sort of protection. That only fueled demand for a Colt.

Then came rumblings of the impending Civil War. He hated war, and as a Northerner, he would only sell guns to the Union. Doing so, he sold hundreds of thousands of guns in the years heading up to the Civil War.

At this point, Colt was one of the richest men in all of America, a millionaire many times over. He had held to his vision, and it proved to be exactly what he knew it could be.

The End of the Line

In the middle of all this, Colt married Elizabeth Jarvis in 1856. They went on a six-month honeymoon to Europe where he wined and dined with various kings and queens, then returned to Hartford and built a massive castle-like home for his wife and family.

You know it must be a big place when the house has a name. It was called Armsmear, perched on a hill that overlooked his armory.

They had five children together, but sadly, every one of them died young. One was stillborn, two died in infancy, one made it to age three, and only one grew to adulthood. The oldest, Caldwell, after attending Yale, working at the Colt factory, and being a successful yachtsman, drowned at age 35 in Charlotte Harbor just off Punta Gorda, Florida, in 1894.

All their children were buried in a private plot on their Armsmear property. Colt himself would be buried there. With the death of Caldwell, Elizabeth moved all of them (her husband and five children) to Cedar Hill Cemetery there in Hartford.

Colt died at his Armsmear mansion in 1862 at the age of 47 from inflammatory arthritis or gout, which is often called the "rich man's disease" because it is associated with the consumption of alcohol, sweet drinks, and other foods that usually only the rich have in sufficient quantities. However, this isn't entirely true, for genetics also plays a big part in whether someone has gout or not.

If I could have grabbed Colt before his death, I would have asked him several business-related questions, such as:

1. Not every company has products that can be produced with interchangeable parts, but most companies would benefit by thinking that way. What business advice would you give a company that really needs to see their work through the eye of interchangeable parts?

2. Without War, do you think your Colt company could have made it?

3. What would you have done if there was no need for guns or underwater mines?

When Colt died, his capable superintendent, Elisha Root, kept everything humming along. By that time, the gun business was so big that it didn't need Colt for it to continue growing. Orders rolled in, even from Europe.

More and more new and improved Colt models were produced. Elizabeth eventually brought in her brother, Richard Jarvis, when Root died a few years later. Together, they ran the Colt company through the Civil War, employing more than 1,000 people at their armory.

The Colt company would continue to create guns that were used in every war and every conflict around the globe. It was often considered to be the gun that tamed the Wild West. Since that fateful day that Texas Ranger Samuel Walker came with his request for 1,000 pistols, effectively giving Colt a second chance at success, millions upon millions of Colts have been produced.

For decades, Elizabeth used her money and influence to help children, soldiers, and the suffragette movement. In 1901, four years before her death, she sold the Colt company to a group of investors. The Colt company is still going today.

66 God created man, and Sam Colt made them equal. 99

– OLD WEST ADAGE

Elizabeth died in 1905 at age 78. She had buried her husband and all of her children. In her death, she joined them at the Cedar Hill Cemetery. Incidentally, the same cemetery is also the final resting place of J. P. Morgan and Katherine Hepburn.

According to her will, more than 100 acres from the Armsmear property was given to the city of Hartford. It's called Colt Park. Legendary author Mark Twain was a regular at Colt Park.

As for their Armsmear mansion, it became a home for women. It is still that today, providing senior women with a beautiful place to stay. Not many senior living facilities can boast of being a mansion!

Samuel Colt was a man who just wouldn't take "no" for an answer. He kept going, he kept fighting, and he kept believing. We as a nation benefited from that.

Samuel Colt
1814–1862

Samuel Morse
1791–1872

Samuel Colt and Samuel Morse met in New York City while they were both busy with their own inventions. They shared practical know-how, and each benefited. Colt's experience with waterproof wire was especially helpful to Morse. Each played a part in taming the Wild West and America's expansion.

CHAPTER 11

Samuel Morse

1791–1872

Maybe you have been told, "You don't get paid to think" or "It's above your pay grade" or "Stick with what you know" or something else along those lines. The fact is, every great invention began as a mere idea. I firmly believe that billionaires and trillionaires are walking around today, just a single thought away from greatness.

Just so you know, you do get paid to think! Don't believe anyone who tells you otherwise.

Samuel Morse is one such man. He worked, and worked hard, but he always kept his eyes and ears tuned into the frequency of creativity and opportunity. Those who listen to that station know what I'm talking about.

Morse was born in Charleston, Massachusetts, now a suburb of Boston, in 1791. His father, Jedidiah, was a preacher, teacher, and geographer. In fact, his *Geography Made Easy* was published in 1784, the year after Noah Webster published his "blue-back speller," and for similar reasons. The young American generation had no clue what America really looked like geographically speaking, so Jedidiah's book helped remedy that.

Sadly, though we have no excuse today, most Americans (regardless of age) are geographically challenged. Many actually believe that Alaska and Hawaii are down below California. I mean, that is where they are often put on maps, but come on!

When Morse was born, George Washington was president, the Louisiana Purchase was still 20 years away, and the newly formed United States basically ended at the Mississippi River. Simply crossing the whole country, much less being able to send a telegram from one side of the country to another, was virtually impossible.

So much would change in one lifetime!

The Man Behind Morse Code

Morse attended Yale College in New Haven, Connecticut, at the age of 15. He showed an interest in science, especially electricity, which was still greatly unknown, even though Benjamin Franklin had been playing around with his kite in an electrical storm almost 60 years earlier.

What really interested him the most was painting. His parents were not impressed with that fact.

He graduated from Yale in 1810—he was only 19 years old—and got a job with a book publisher back in Boston. Maybe his father's experience with books and publishing helped land his first job, but Morse was bored. Painting was much more interesting.

> 66 I gave my heart to the Americans and thought of nothing else but raising my banner and adding my colors to theirs. 99
>
> – MARQUIS DE LAFAYETTE

A local famous painter, Washington Allston, was teaching in London, England, and young Morse probably asked or maybe even begged his parents to let him go to England and learn from this master. They agreed, and off Morse went, his first trip of many across the ocean. He would be there for four years.

While in England, the War of 1812 happened. It was again, and for the last time, England against the United States. Morse was very patriotic by the time he returned home.

Unfortunately for well-trained and artistically talented Morse, nobody cared. He couldn't find a job painting what he wanted. Instead, he went back to painting what people were willing to pay for—portraits.

At painting portraits, Morse was very good. So that's what he did. He traveled up and down the country, painting mostly portraits for basically anyone who would hire him. In the South, thanks to the cotton gin, money was flowing and he found a lot of wealthy customers who would commission a painting. (Today, some of his paintings sell for more than $1,000,000, so if you happen to have a family heirloom painting by Morse, you should get it appraised.)

At age 27, he married Lucretia Walker. They would have five children, with two dying in infancy. Home was in New Haven, Connecticut, but he would spend his winters in the South, painting as many portraits as he could.

In 1825, Morse was in Washington, D.C., painting a portrait of the famous Marquis de Lafayette, who played a tremendous role in the American Revolution alongside George Washington. This was the last time that Lafayette would come to America, and Morse had been paid $1,000 to paint it. This was huge for him!

As he was painting, a messenger arrived with a letter. His wife was sick. He couldn't drop what he was doing and rush home.

66 Whenever the pillars of Christianity shall be overthrown, our present republican forms of government, and all blessings which flow from them, must fall with them. 99

– JEDIDIAH MORSE

After all, it was 300 miles from D.C., back to New Haven, Connecticut, and a trip that would probably take him a week at best.

The next day, another letter arrived. His wife was dead and already buried! She had been laid to rest in the Grove Street Cemetery beside their two dead children.

They say this was the moment that Morse first began to really think about being able to communicate more quickly than word of mouth, mail, stagecoach, or ship. I can understand why.

And if you wanted to "rush" a message to England, it would take you at least 10 days. People can die and be buried, and wars can be won or lost in that amount of time.

For Morse, this was the worst of times. Consider this:

- 1821: baby Elizabeth Ann Morse died
- 1822: baby Lucretia Ann Morse died
- 1825: wife Lucretia (age 25) died
- 1826: father Jedediah died
- 1828: mother Elizabeth died

He left his children with family members and went back to Europe. He needed time to reflect, process, and paint. Totally understandable, but I'm not sure three years away from his kids was the best move.

While in Europe, there were experiments going on with electromagnets, wires, and communication in some manner. Nothing was very clear, but the idea was churning in a lot of scientific minds.

In 1832, Morse decided it was time to return to America. On board his ship was Charles T. Jackson, a doctor and scientist, and they would have many discussions about science, trends, and electromagnets.

Morse's brain must have been spinning, and he must have never forgotten his wife's passing and his desire to communicate quickly across long distances, because he drew diagrams, wrote notes to himself, and basically conceived the whole idea for the telegraph while sailing home!

Morse settled in New York and became an arts and design professor at today's New York University. He also worked tirelessly on his telegraph idea.

Creating the Telegraph

To get a little perspective, the telephone wouldn't be invented until 1876, four years after Morse died. So, from 1844 when Morse sent his famous first telegraph message until 1876, if you wanted to communicate long distance, you used the telegraph. That was it. There was nothing else.

What Morse envisioned, he began to build. Over the next five years, he went through countless versions, drafts, attempts, and failures. His initial models were complex, with multiple cogs, wires, magnets, and paper, but they did work.

At that point, after reading about Morse's work, Alfred Vail approached Morse with a few ways to improve his creation. Vail was also an inventor, had some money, and could get his fingers on the machine parts that Morse might need. He was the ideal partner to have. (Vail died in 1859, mostly forgotten by the world for his role with Morse.)

Feeling the telegraph was at a point it could be patented, Morse applied for a patent in 1837. He also tried to get permission to experiment with his telegraph between Baltimore, Maryland, and Washington, D.C. It was only a 40-mile stretch, but I think Morse was trying to "own" the territory. I don't think he knew just how big his telegraph would become! There was no need to own a territory, for the whole world would soon want what he had.

In need of more funding, he again went to Europe. Two years later, he was back and still without any financial backers. During that time, he did revamp his Morse alphabet. He scrapped his original plan of using whole words, as that quickly became too cumbersome, and chose instead to use only letters. Any word could then be spelled, using dots and dashes that matched each letter. Much cleaner and much faster, the Morse Code that we know and use today was born.

Every step of the way, Morse maintained the less-is-more approach. His eventual goal was to communicate through a single wire. He eventually did, and that was part of what made everything work.

After years of continual improvement and continual pressuring of Congress, in 1843, he finally received enough money ($30,000 from the government) to roll out his telegraph to the world. This was the moment he had sacrificed for, waited for, and worked for.

Would it work?

Within a year, he had wire running from Washington, D.C., to Baltimore, Maryland. Most of it was above ground on poles. They tried underground at first, but that didn't work as well. For crossing water ways, Samuel Colt had already worked with Morse to perfect that part of the equation.

On May 24, 1844, it was show time!

66 Every child has a dream, to pursue the dream is in every child's hand to make it a reality. One's invention is another's tool. 99

– SAMUEL MORSE

Morse was in the US Supreme Court building, and Vail was in the Baltimore, Maryland, railroad depot 40 miles away. Morse tapped out a message to Vail, and Vail sent it back. It read the same going and coming, "What hath God wrought." The message was quick and accurate.

Always into the little details, Morse gave the honor of creating the first telegraphed message to someone else. He let the daughter of his friend, Henry Ellsworth, who was Commissioner of the US Patent Office and who had helped him finally get his US patent, craft the first telegram. Annie, age 17, chose "What hath God wrought" from Deuteronomy in the Old Testament.

At that moment, history was made.

To say that things took off from there would be a great understatement! News spread like wildfire. With the Magnetic

Telegraph Company formed and patents in place, everything surged forward.

Unfortunately, almost at the same speed of telegraph wires being strung up everywhere, so did the costly battle to keep his patents in place begin. Other individuals and companies that had created similar telegraphs, but none as good or that used a single wire, fought him left and right.

Remember that voyage home in 1832 when Morse and Dr. Charles Jackson talked about electromagnets? It's a good thing Morse took notes, because years later, of course *after* Morse had received his patent for the telegraph, Jackson claimed that the telegraph was his idea.

Jackson had the nasty habit of laying claim to someone else's breakthrough and claiming it as his own. He did it to several other prominent figures. But still, it took Morse time to find witnesses from the voyage (many years after the trip occurred), put his old notes together, and argue his case.

Telegraph wires were being strung up between every big city in the US, and within a few years, his telegraph became the standard across Europe. No need to "own" territory when it's all yours!

He had the patents, but do you think he received credit?

Nope!

And royalties?

Hardly!

His company was growing rapidly, but the legal battles were constant.

In 1853, Morse ended up taking his patent-rights case all the way to the Supreme Court! He won his case, thankfully. I think that the way Eli Whitney was mistreated after creating the earth-shattering cotton gin probably helped Morse win. That, and the fact that Morse's telegraph used only one wire.

As a result of Morse being officially declared the inventor, quite a few European countries that had been using his technology "royalty free" for years decided they would pay him a royalty. Many also gave him awards and honors, but most importantly, they collectively coughed up what amounted to about $2,000,000 in today's money.

After living a life that would admittedly be considered cash strapped or just plain poor, Morse was finally a wealthy man.

Connecting the World

Morse remarried in 1848. His first wife had died 23 years earlier and all their children were grown up. His second wife, Sarah Griswold, was 26 years old. He was 57. She was a great encouragement to him and his work. They had four children together, all of whom lived into adulthood. She would outlive him by almost 30 years.

Interestingly, Sarah was deaf. Maybe they used sign language or she could read lips, but I can imagine Morse sending his kids Morse Code messages at the dinner table without her knowing. He was the inventor of Morse Code; how could he not teach his children? If that didn't happen, I'd be surprised. I would have done it!

Morse bought the Locust Grove estate, 75 miles straight north up the Hudson River from New York City. If you make it to Locust Grove (a national historic landmark) in Poughkeepsie, New York, today, you'll enjoy the mansion, miles of walking trails, and landscaped gardens, all on 200 acres that overlook the Hudson River. Amazing!

But Morse did not retire. Far from it. Sure, Locust Grove was ideal for his kids and grandkids, but he had much work to do.

The telegraph soon covered the East Coast, but it would take several more years before it reached all the way to California. When it finally happened in 1861, the legendary Pony Express delivery service instantly became a thing of the past. They could hardly saddle a horse by the time a message was received. That pretty much defines "obsolete." Eventually, even the telegraph would be outmoded, but Morse Code would rule the world for many years to come.

What about connecting wires from the US to England? Could it be done? The need was there, as anything was better than the usual "expedited" 10-day journey.

Apparently, there were people who thought laying a continuous cable for 2,500 miles (basically the width of the US from coast to coast) was doable and financially viable. In 1856, work began, funds were raised, cable was made and insulated, and ships began the precarious task of making it happen.

Morse played a part, using his experience and expertise (some of which he gained from Samuel Colt) to assist in the project.

66 Everything great in science and art is simple. What can be less complicated than the greatest discoveries of humanity—gravitation, the compass, the printing press, the steam engine, the electric telegraph? 99

– JULES VERNE

It was an incredible undertaking that took years of work, but they pulled it off! In 1858, Queen Victoria had the honor of sending the world's first telegraph across an entire ocean, and she did so with a message to President James Buchanan.

Naturally, the world was abuzz with the news! Unfortunately, that cable would quit working within a few weeks. But human ingenuity would rule the day, for more and more new and improved cable laying attempts were done over the coming years, until sending a telegram across the ocean became a common occurrence.

Amazingly, these telegraph stations at either end would remain in service all the way up until 1965. Almost 100 years of continuous communication would take place along those many cables! Today, the oceans are laced with countless fiber optic cables. We had to start somewhere, and Morse's copper telegraph wires were where it all began.

Morse officially retired in 1871 in New York City. It would be a party like none other. After a parade, harbor cruise, and statue unveiling, they held the world's first live group chat!

Somehow, telegraph stations from around the world were connected to telegraph operators at his celebration party. These operators sent them all, in every corner of the world, a simultaneous message that read:

"Greetings and thanks to the telegraph fraternity throughout the world. Glory to God in the highest, on earth peace, goodwill to men."

Morse, age 79, sat down and tapped out his name to complete the message:

"S.F.B. Morse"

What a grand finale! The whole world received his farewell message, and all at the same time.

Officially retired and out of the public eye, Morse spent time with his family, gave generously to causes (colleges, churches, seminaries, missions, etc.), and even supported a few starving artists who probably reminded him of himself many years earlier.

In 1872, Morse died of pneumonia. He was 80 years old. He was buried in the Green-Wood Cemetery in Brooklyn, New York. His wife, Sarah, would join him in 1901.

Morse was responsible for connecting the entire world together, for the first time ever, with technology that allowed for almost instant communication. That affected trade, wars, governments, language, science, business, families, and everything in between.

He also brought employment to an untold number of people (including even Thomas Edison, who worked for a time as a telegraph operator) across the nation and around the world.

Just as Eli Whitney didn't think his cotton gin would make such an impact, I don't think Morse expected his telegraph to have the impact that it did.

If you ever happen to be in Washington, D.C., at the Rotunda of the US Capitol Building, look up at the domed ceiling. You will see many important figures there, but where the rainbow comes down on the left, you will see three figures of importance in the field of science: Benjamin Franklin, Robert Fulton, and yours truly, Samuel Morse.

Or if you are in Central Park in New York City, one of the east entrances has a statue of Morse with his famous telegraph machine. It was unveiled in 1871 with him in attendance.

Or if you make it to the Smithsonian, you can see his original 1837 telegraph equipment in the Museum of American History.

Or if you are more serious, join one of the many Morse Code clubs that are in existence around the world. Learn it, and then teach your children. You'll be sure to have fun at the dinner table!

If I could have asked Morse a few questions, I would have wanted to know a few things, including:

1. If you knew your telegraph would change the world, what would you have done differently?

2. Did you ever dream in Morse Code?

3. What was your biggest wish for your telegraph? Did you want to speed up communication for one specific reason more than any other?

4. What's the fastest way to learn Morse Code?

I'm sure that millions of deaths and millions of births were reported over Morse's telegraph. I would say he certainly made up for the fact that he heard so slowly about his wife's death.

Believe it or not, Morse Code was used commercially until 1999. And the last message they sent? It was the same as the first:

"What hath God wrought."

What a fitting tribute to world changer, Samuel Morse.

Samuel Morse **Theodore Judah**
1791–1872   1826–1863

As Samuel Morse rode trains throughout New York, Massachusetts, and Connecticut, he may have ridden a train on one of the lines that Theodore Judah was responsible for, but it was the telegraph that bonded their work together. Train tracks and telegraph poles were inseparable, especially out West. When Judah's transcontinental railroad was finally completed, a one-word telegraph message alerted the entire nation.

CHAPTER 12

Theodore Judah

1826-1863

Though telegraph wires had been put up that connected the nation from coast to coast, there was still no quick, safe mode of transportation across the country. Sure, the Pony Express riders could do it in a few days, avoiding Indians and using all their relay stations along the way, but for the people going west, it was horseback or wagon.

Yes, you could take a boat around the bottom of South America, but that was also slow. The typical journey by land or boat would take you four to six months. That's slow going!

What America needed was a train track from coast to coast. But with mountain range after mountain range, as previous settlers and explorers (including Lewis and Clark) had found, such a venture was nigh to impossible.

A telegraph wire with its telegraph poles could go straight up and over a mountain. But trains have very strict limits. The biggest is gradient, as in, how steep the incline is for the track. The gradient must be minimal for the engine to be able to pull the train up the hill and to maintain speed while coming down the hill.

Specifically, gradient is defined by how many feet you go up or down every 100 feet. So, for example, if the train track goes up or down one foot over a 100-foot stretch of track, then you have a 1 percent gradient. And a 2 percent gradient was decided to be about max for a track.

That means you need to find a lot of flat or almost flat places through hills, canyons, and mountains (often 12,000–14,000 feet in height), which is clearly not happening! The best approach is usually to run the track right beside a river, and then bore through the mountain if necessary.

What's more, any track that curves must have a lesser gradient because curved track decreases the power of the engines and increases the risk of tipping over.

And on top of that, these were steam engines, and steam engines ran on coal. So, if you ran a train through a tunnel, you instantly had a choking hazard! Nobody, especially someone traveling in first class, wants to asphyxiate while in a dark tunnel.

By 1861, when the telegraph finally connected the nation from coast to coast, not many western states were even states yet. California was added in 1850 and Oregon in 1859, but Nevada, Colorado, Montana, Washington, Idaho, Wyoming, Utah, among others, were still territories. It was rough, not very populated, and dangerous.

No wonder putting a train line across the country had never been done before!

In situations or projects like these, you need someone who is crazy enough to even try it.

Enter the right man for the job, Theodore Judah, also known as "Crazy Judah." Many thought he had a few screws loose, but he believed a transcontinental railroad could be done.

Believing in a Train Track Across America

Whoever came up with the term "one-track mind" probably knew Theodore Judah, for trains were pretty much all that Judah thought about.

Judah was born in Bridgeport, Connecticut, a town less than 20 miles from New Haven, Connecticut, and directly on the route from New Haven to New York, Philadelphia, and Washington, D.C. The likes of Samuel Morse, Samuel Colt, and Noah Webster would have passed regularly through Bridgeport.

When Judah's father died, young Judah (around 12 or 13 at the time) became an assistant to a land surveyor. That was probably grunt work at the lowest level, but Judah excelled in all things related to engineering. His love was trains and would quickly show how capable he was.

66 In purely engineering retrospect, Judah's achievements would seem nothing short of providential, especially in comparison to modern route surveying efforts. 99

– J. David Rogers and Charles R. Spinks

He studied engineering in school and worked on a short train line that ran beside the Mohawk River in eastern New York. Then he worked on a bigger train line that ran the 60 miles from Springfield, Massachusetts, (where the publisher of the Merriam-Webster dictionary was located) north to Brattleboro, Vermont. Then he worked on the Springfield to New Haven, Connecticut, line, which was also about 60 miles in length.

By age 20, he was a chief engineer's assistant, which was a lot less grunt work than assistant to a mere surveyor. Judah was learning all the parts of the equation, a necessary skill for what was to come.

The next year (1847), Judah married Anna Pierce. She quickly found that she had married the railroad! "Time, money, brains, strength, body and soul were absorbed," she noted when later describing his never-ending focus on the railway.

There were thousands upon thousands of miles of train track running up and down the East Coast, but there was nothing out West.

Judah proved his value by coming up with a workable solution to a train line running from the Niagara area to the Great Lakes. He knew his business and found solutions, quickly becoming chief engineer himself of a New York train line.

California was trying to build a train line within the Sacramento Valley. Judah was recruited, traveled (with Anna) to California, and did the survey work while others raised the necessary funds. The track was finished successfully the next year and was recognized as the first train track west of the Mississippi.

He was chief engineer for several more lines in California, solidifying his position as the go-to-guy for trains on the West Coast.

All the while, Judah was thinking of the transcontinental track. He studied the land and talked to the locals. Perhaps he saw just how high the mountains were out West. Either way, he knew that building a track from coast to coast could only be done with the help of politicians.

It was way too big of an undertaking otherwise. It was no regional endeavor. It was national, and even at that, it was on a scale that had never been accomplished before.

Extensive surveys were conducted during that time, and the findings were presented to Congress. Congress debated, asked questions, and pretty much kicked the can down the road.

Meanwhile, the western territories and states were getting more restless. They wanted a track laid to connect them with the rest of America.

Doing their necessary due diligence, Judah and others explored and surveyed possible routes from the Sacramento Valley east through the Sierra Nevada mountains, and with a gradient of only 1 percent. He found a way through Donner Pass, one of the hurdles to crossing the Sierra Nevada range.

Judah again returned to Congress, and this time Anna showed paintings of some of the areas that Judah had surveyed. She was a painter, and her paintings helped many of the congressional members "see" the land and what the process would include.

Building a Train Track Across America

Interestingly, in 1845, 20 years after Eli Whitney died, a distant cousin of his, Asa Whitney, made an official presentation to Congress for a railroad that would cross the nation. The timing wasn't right and Congress didn't approve of his plan, but it seems that the ability to see into the future might flow through the Whitney blood.

66 A man who has never gone to school may steal from a freight car; but if he has a university education, he may steal the whole railroad. 99

– THEODORE ROOSEVELT

The very next year, about 80 settlers on their way to California got stuck in an unexpected snowstorm on their way over the Sierra Nevada mountains. Almost 50 percent of them died, and many of the bodies were eaten by those who lived to tell about it. The mountain pass they came through was named after them, Donner Pass.

Both unfortunately and fortunately for Judah, everything that lead up to the Civil War affected his train track. The bad news was that it slowed down the initial decision-making (and made finding workers much more difficult), but the good news was that the Republican Congress could make decisions without the Democratic southern states that had left the Union. President Abraham Lincoln approved the Pacific Railroad Act of 1862.

It was finally happening!

There would be two tracks being laid simultaneously, one going west and one going east. They would meet somewhere in the middle. The track heading east was the Central Pacific Railroad (with Judah as the chief engineer) and the other heading west was the Union Pacific Railroad.

The Central Pacific line began at Judah's line in the Sacramento Valley. It offered direct access to the Pacific Ocean. Connecting to the Union Pacific branch would open trade and transportation directly from one ocean to the other, something that had never been done in the history of North America.

The Union Pacific line began at the furthest westerly train station, and that was in Council Bluffs, Iowa, on the western edge of the state, right on the banks of the Missouri River. Lewis and Clark had gone up and down the Missouri 60 years earlier, long before the city was established and long before anyone was thinking about train tracks.

The Central Pacific line was funded by investors who believed in the vision, and who stood to gain by the profits from the building process, as well as the business that would naturally follow after the tracks were in services. They were not train men.

> 66 What a man does for himself, dies with him. What a man does for his community lives long after he's gone. 99
>
> – THEODORE ROOSEVELT

Of those investors and decision-makers, Judah was one of them. He had some money, but he mostly had the necessary know-how and the uncanny ability to get a job done. He was clearly the leader behind the Central Pacific line, and those in Washington, D.C., saw him as that. He was a good partner to have.

During the rest of 1862 and into 1863, the investors and Judah butted heads. Judah was detailed (he certainly had to be in his profession) and believed his approach was best. It ruffled his feathers when the non-train investors told him how to do his job.

He, in turn, made them upset by his unwavering focus on building his portion of the track and not on making as much money as possible along the way.

At one point, the California investors paid a geologist to lie, saying there were hills where there were flatlands. Since each train line was paid by the government for previously agreed upon factors, such as rivers (a bridge is needed), mountains (a trestle or tunned is needed), or flatlands (the cheapest option), there were plenty of opportunities to pad their pockets.

This happens all the time today. That doesn't make it right, but it is a common occurrence. I've seen pharmaceutical, energy, and investment companies, just to name a few, hire people to create completely bogus reports, all to make money, avoid lawsuits, or gain government approval for something.

In truth, the costs for the Central Pacific line were much higher than originally estimated, but lying to raise profits didn't sit well with Judah. When the investors' plan with the geologist was about to bring in a more money, Judah stopped it.

He probably told the truth, which uncovered the investors. Maybe they were tired of Judah. Either way, the investors made their move, basically forcing him and other like-minded investors to either pay up or leave. Judah used his stock options to stay on the board, but several of his friends were forced out.

What the big California investors may not have known was that Judah had an option to buy them all out. He just needed investors, and he had them back in New York.

He sent telegraphs to New York and set it up. He probably knew this was his only opportunity to do so. If he didn't buy them out now, they would surely find a way to kick him out.

If I could have grabbed Judah's attention away from his surveys, maps, and calculations just for a moment, I would have liked to ask him one question:

You can arrange for new investors to buy out the current investors via telegraph. Do you really need to travel in person to New York City?

In October of 1863, with the Central Pacific line steadily moving forward, Judah and Anna boarded a steamship headed south from San Francisco, California. Instead of crossing the Central American country of Nicaragua as they had done before, they sailed a little farther south to cross in Panama. It was a much shorter distance across land, and as of 1855, there was a train line that ran from coast to coast.

At some point on his journey across Panama, he was bitten by a mosquito that carried yellow fever.

Back in those days, yellow fever was incredibly dangerous, mostly because nobody knew what caused it. Bloodletting and forced vomiting were often recommended! In my books, that alone would kill you, but that was part of the regimen in Philadelphia in 1793 when yellow fever killed 10 percent of the city's population! More than 5,000 people died.

Yellow fever is a virus that causes the typical fever and chills, but it can also deepen to where it damages the liver, causing the person to basically bleed out. The vaccine from 1937 is still in use today, and even with that, thousands of people die each year from yellow fever.

As the steamship headed north through the Caribbean and up the East Coast, Judah got sicker and sicker. The day after they arrived back in New York City, he died. He was only 37 years old.

Anna had Judah buried back home in Greenfield, Massachusetts. They had no children. All they had was the railroad, as that was what Judah lived for, and that didn't treat him well in the end.

When the two train lines eventually met in 1869, Anna described that day by saying, "It seemed as though the spirit of my brave husband descended upon me and together we were there unseen, unheard of by man."

To add insult to injury, or perhaps as a sign that Judah was still in control, the date the trains came together was May 10th, Anna's wedding anniversary! She and Judah would have been married 20 years at that point.

The California investors would get wealthy by the Central Pacific line and Judah's name was thrown in the mud. Anna grieved to see the injustice, and she did all she could to defend her Judah.

Eventually, Collis Huntington, the leader of the California investors behind the Central Pacific line who butted heads with Judah, was seen for being the manipulative person that he was. He regularly gave bribes to politicians (just as is done today) and many people hated him. He died in 1900, very wealthy.

When Anna died in 1895, she was buried with Judah in her family plot. If you visit the Federal Street Cemetery in Greenfield, Massachusetts, you'll find their cement tomb with big "Pierce" letters on it, which is her last name.

Connecting the Train Track Across America

The Central Pacific line continued its slow eastward advance without Judah. It was hard going. Literally! They had to chip through solid granite, and it slowed progress to about one foot per day!

Of the 19 tunnels that were part of the transcontinental railroad, 15 of them were on the Central Pacific line. I've seen some of the bridges and trestles they built out of wood, crossing rivers and skirting cliffs, and I'm amazed that they could build it, as well as run a heavy train across it.

To me, their work is definitely up there with the great wonders of the world!

It was hard to find workers out West to help with the track laying. Most of the people there were settlers or miners looking for gold and they had no intention of stopping what they were doing. In short, there were not that many people around looking for a job.

As a result, the Central Pacific line began to look to outside labor. Thousands of Chinese had come to California looking for gold or to start a new life. Many were soon hired to be part of the round-the-clock (three shifts each day, seven days a week) crew putting down tracking, digging tunnels, building bridges and trestles, and hammering spikes. As much as 90 percent of the total work force ended up being Chinese.

On the Union Pacific side, their workers were primarily Irish immigrants and Civil War veterans. The Civil War ran from

1861 to 1865, and any veterans looking for work would be on the eastern side.

The east-going Central Pacific line would cover a distance of almost 700 miles, while the west-going Union Pacific line was longer at almost 1,100 miles. More than 1,500 workers died in the process due to explosions, freezing temperatures, avalanches, Indian attacks, and disease.

It took six years to complete! That is an incredibly long time, and they were working around the clock. The entire project was of gargantuan proportions.

Near the end, with both crews working on flatter land, it was a race each day to see how many miles of track they could put down. It must have been a great feeling for the engineers and workers to be able to lay down several miles of track in a day after struggling through mountains and ravines that had slowed their progress to a mere crawl.

> 66 May God continue the unity of our Country as this Railroad unites the two great Oceans of the world. 99
>
> – Inscribed on the golden last spike

Once they knew they were getting close, President Ulysses S. Grant chose a point where the east-going and west-going train tracks would meet. It would be Promontory Summit, Utah.

Promontory, Utah, is north of the Great Salt Lake and is still out in the middle of nowhere. Its claim to fame is May 10, 1869, when the tracks met.

Sadly, neither the person who dreamed it (Theodore Judah) nor the person who approved it (Abraham Lincoln) lived to see it completed. Interestingly, Samuel Morse did. He was still alive, and it was his telegraph that announced to the world that the transcontinental railroad was complete. The telegraph office at Promontory Summit, Utah, sent a telegraph across the nation that simply read:

DONE!

And it was.

Not only was history made, but the nation would soon change. It was connected for the first time. Months and months of dangerous travel across the wilderness or sailing around South America or cutting across Central America could suddenly be safely done in a single week by train. Imagine that!

Business could be conducted, settlers could move at higher levels, and supplies could be transported with ease. The entire US economy surged forward, thanks to the transcontinental railroad!

Truly, the western expansion that Thomas Jefferson had pushed for was finally happening. Jefferson died in 1826, the year Theodore Judah was born.

> 66 The close relationship between railroad expansion and the general development and prosperity of the country is nowhere brought more distinctly into relief than in connection with the construction of the Pacific railroads. 99
>
> – JOHN MOODY

Just as Judah envisioned, linking the nation by train benefited the nation in countless ways. It no doubt saved a lot of lives. It would have saved his, had he been able to travel to New York City via train instead of going across Panama as he and Anna did.

Eventually, the Panama Canal itself would be finished, but it wouldn't be completed until 1914. In the process, thousands of workers died of yellow fever. That was a whole lot better than the French. They had tried to complete the canal 20 years earlier, but yellow fever just destroyed them.

The original Walter Reed did figure out in 1901 that mosquitoes were the source of yellow fever, and that knowledge helped incredibly the men building the Panama Canal, but it wouldn't be until 1937 that South African scientist Max Theiler came up with a vaccine. Too bad all of that was no help to Judah.

The next time you are walking down Judah Street in San Francisco, California, or climbing Mount Judah near Donner Peak in California's Tahoe National Forest, you now know where the name came from.

Eventually, no doubt others would have stepped forward to push for a transcontinental railway line. It was inevitable. The nation was growing and trains would eventually be everywhere, but Theodore Judah was the right man at the right time. He played an integral part in getting the process started and through some of the logistical hurdles.

If only he could have lived to tell about it.

Theodore Judah **Ulysses S. Grant**
1826–1863   1822–1885

Theodore Judah started the east-going railway line of the transcontinental railroad, and it was Ulysses S. Grant who chose where the two lines would meet. They both crossed the Isthmus of Panama out of necessity. Years later, Grant rode the train line that Judah died trying to build.

CHAPTER 13

Ulysses S. Grant

1822-1885

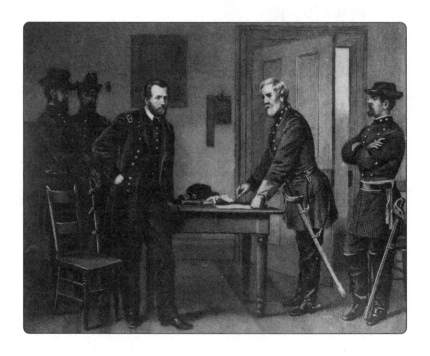

Most people know Ulysses S. Grant by his face, which is on the $50 bill. Who he was, what he believed in, what he accomplished for the United States, and the fact that he was our 18th president is why he graces our currency.

Born in Point Pleasant, Ohio, which sits on the Ohio River separating Ohio from Kentucky, and then raised 20 miles east in Georgetown, Ohio, Grant grew up with a father who was a tradesman, a Republican, and an abolitionist. It would be a good foundation for what was to come in Grant's life.

Tanning was his father's profession, and Grant hated it. He preferred working with horses or farming. So, with an aversion for the family business, and no real goal of his own, young Grant was sent to the United States Military Academy at West Point, New York.

Not just anyone could go to West Point, but Grant was nominated. Interestingly, someone messed up his name during his initial registration process. Instead of being Hiram Ulysses Grant, he was listed as Ulysses S. Grant. The only way he could attend school was if he changed his name to match the roster, which he did. The "S" never actually stood for anything.

West Point is on the Hudson River, just north of New York City. Grant graduated in 1843. He was a fair student, good at math, but excellent with horses. If he had taken a steamboat up the river just 30 miles, which he might have done, he would have arrived at the Locust Grove estate, which Samuel Morse purchased and moved into with his family just a few years later.

Grant's big plan after school was to complete the required four years of military duty, then become a math teacher. Thankfully, that small dream never had a chance to be fulfilled.

From West Point, Grant was posted in St. Louis, Missouri. It was from this point that Lewis and Clark had started their expedition just 39 years earlier. Clark had just died in St. Louis only five years before Grant was stationed there.

While in St. Louis, Grant met his future wife, Julia Dent. In 1845, he finally had permission from Julia's father to marry her, but then the Mexican-American War broke out, and they wouldn't get married until 1848 after the war.

Coming from St. Louis to fight in the Mexican-American War, he no doubt knew fellow soldiers Meriwether Lewis Clark (William Clark's son) and Jean Baptiste (Sacajawea's son), as both hailed from St. Louis as well.

Grant showed boldness and valor during the war, though his role was a minor one. He also was not a fan of the war, for he felt it was completely unnecessary. He served under General Zachary Taylor, who went on to become the 12th president. Interestingly, another soldier by the name of Samuel Walker of the famed Walker Colt that Samuel Colt created as requested, also served under Zachary Taylor.

After the war, Grant and Julia did get married, but he didn't resign from the military just yet. He was sent in 1850 out West to help maintain law and order. The gold rush of 1849 and subsequent years had created massive migration of people, so a presence of soldiers at Fort Vancouver in the Oregon Territory on the Columbia River (the very river that Lewis and Clark traversed) was needed to keep mining and related trade safe and uninterrupted.

Because there was no transcontinental railway in place yet, going to and from California with all their equipment meant a four- to six-month trip down around South America or a one- to two-month via a Central American country. They ended up going via steamship to Panama, crossing over by mule, and then getting another steamship north. Grant lost more than 100 men due to cholera. He was lucky to make it across and live to tell about it.

He spent two years in the West dabbling in a few business ventures, none of which panned out.

> 66 The art of war is simple enough. Find out where your enemy is. Get at him as soon as you can. Strike him as hard as you can, and keep moving on. 99
>
> - ULYSSES S. GRANT

When Grant had married Julia, her father had given him 80 acres. That was certainly a nice gift! In 1854, Grant finally resigned from the military and settled down to life on a farm. Or at least, he tried to. He wasn't the best at it, but it was the economic downturn of the US economy in 1857 that put an end to his farming plans. He ended up selling firewood on the streets of St. Louis just to put food on the table.

Unable to provide for his wife and four children, Grant did what he most disliked—he went back to work in his father's tanning business. He tended the family store. They eked out a living, but it was not a happy time.

Fighting in the Civil War

When the Civil War started, the Union was busy recruiting. President Abraham Lincoln wanted leaders who were loyal and believed in the cause. As an abolitionist and an experienced soldier, Grant certainly fit the bill. He rejoined in 1861 as a colonel. He was back in uniform, the one profession that he had always been good at.

Not wasting any time, Grant led his men from Illinois down into northern Tennessee and attacked Fort Donelson on the Cumberland River. Situated just 75 miles from Nashville, which also sits on the Cumberland River, the fort was an important defense of Nashville. Grant took the fort, capturing more than 10,000 Confederate soldiers in the process.

The Confederate General at Fort Donelson, Simon Buckner, happened to be one of Grant's old friends. They had both gone to West Point together and had fought in the Mexican-American War together.

No doubt Buckner thought his negotiations for surrender would in some way be special. They were friends and classmates, after all! But Grant's short reply put an end to that dreaming:

"No terms except an unconditional and immediate surrender can be accepted. I propose to move immediately on your works."

This boosted Grant's fame and respect, with some calling him "Unconditional Surrender Grant" as a play on his "U. S. Grant" initials, but it was truly the best way to speed up the war and save lives. (After the war, Buckner went on to become the governor of Kentucky.)

Before the Confederate soldiers were shipped out to a prisoner-of-war camp, Grant offered money to Buckner to help him or his family. This is what made the Civil War so painful. It was friends killing friends, not to mention family killing their own family members. It was brutal.

After taking Fort Donelson, Grant instantly went from being a Colonel to a Major General.

Heading south in Tennessee, Grant's men fought the Battle of Shiloh, one of the deadliest battles of the Civil War. The Union won, but it came at a cost of more than 20,000 American lives (counting both sides, of course).

From there, Grant proceeded to lay siege to the Confederates in Vicksburg, Mississippi. The stakes were high, for whomever controlled Vicksburg controlled trade up and down the Mississippi River. Again, Grant was victorious.

After Vicksburg, Abraham Lincoln wrote a letter to Grant that included these words:

"I write this now as a grateful acknowledgment for the almost inestimable service you have done the country."

From that point on, the Confederate army was on the defense. They did not have the seemingly unending supply of fresh troops, as the Union did, and Grant pressed this advantage at every turn. He was relentless, continually attacking, always attacking.

The Confederate position on Lookout Mountain, in the northwest corner of Georgia and overlooking Chattanooga,

Tennessee, was the next to fall to Grant. At this point, it looked like the Union might have its hero, someone who could finally finish the Civil War for the country.

Grant was brought to Washington, D.C., where he was given the rank of Lieutenant General (the same rank as George Washington) and charge of the entire Union army. It was 1864. The war would soon be over.

From many different fronts, Grant planned constant attacks against Robert E. Lee and his Confederate soldiers. Eventually, Richmond, Virginia, the Confederate capital, fell to Grant.

Days later, Grant and Lee began discussing terms of surrender. On April 9, 1865, in Appomattox, Virginia, 90 miles west of Richmond, General Lee surrendered. The Civil War didn't officially end until the next year, but for most people, this was the end of the Civil War.

When Lee surrendered, Grant was gracious. He allowed the Confederate soldiers, which were his fellow Americans, to return home. They were not prisoners of war. They could take their personal effects, including their horses, back with them. After all, every man needed a horse for farming. Grant also fed them before they left.

Within the week, Abraham Lincoln was shot and killed. The Civil War was over, slavery was abolished, and the nation was in shambles. Grant's next task quickly became that of trying to be a peacemaker.

The southern states, having built much of their economies on slavery, were faced with the massive task of reinventing almost every business, every industry, and virtually every aspect of their society. It would not be easy, and Grant tried to help in every way he could.

In the meantime, Grant's titles kept getting bigger and bigger. He became General of the Federal Army in 1866 and Secretary of War soon after. And then naturally, President of the United States in 1869!

The 18th President

President Ulysses S. Grant is remembered for quickly signing laws that led to the 15th Amendment, which states:

"The right of citizens of the United States to vote shall not be denied or abridged by the United States or by any State on account of race, color, or previous condition of servitude."

A few years into his presidency, the Democrats and Ku Klux Klan (KKK) supremacists tried to gain control of southern states and bring back slavery. Grant squashed that, basically putting the KKK out of business for decades.

All during the Civil War, the transcontinental railway as a dream and then a reality had been under way. President Lincoln saw the railroad as a necessary part of the war effort, but it would prove after the war to be an essential tool for unifying and expanding the nation as a whole.

As president, Grant had the privilege of choosing where the six-year-long project would end. The east-going Central Pacific line that Theodore Judah started and the west-going Union Pacific line were due to meet in May of 1869. Grant chose Promontory, Utah, as the place where the two railway lines would connect.

Julia was a gracious first lady, who not only hosted many events, but she also read mail, attended senate hearings, and helped Grant in his role as president. She enjoyed life in the White House and even hosted their only daughter's wedding there. Not many people can say they got married in the White House, much less while their dad was president!

After two terms as president, during which time Grant had to contend with the Reconstruction efforts, keep England as an ally, broker peace with the American Indians, guarantee equal rights for Black people with the Civil Rights Acts of 1870 and 1875, handle several different foreign situations, and deal with financial issues that came as a result of the Civil War, among many other things, Grant was done with politics and being a soldier.

It was time to retire.

Riding into the Sunset

Grant and Julia's daughter had married an Englishman and was living in England at the time. They planned to sail (take a steamboat, actually) over and vacation with her. But once again, Grant's plans were too little.

““ As soon as slavery fired upon the flag it was felt, we all felt, even those who did not object to slaves, that slavery must be destroyed. We felt that it was a stain to the Union that men should be bought and sold like cattle. There had to be an end of slavery. ””

– Ulysses S. Grant

The trip grew and grew, eventually becoming a world tour that took more than two years to complete. Not only was it a great family adventure, but it turned out to be a diplomatic mission at the same time.

They left Philadelphia, Pennsylvania, bound for England. Upon arrival, it was parades, speeches, tours, and dining with everyone important, including Queen Victoria. Then to multiple countries in Europe where the meeting with dignitaries, swapping war stories with other military leaders, and seeing the sights continued.

From Europe they sailed across the Mediterranean Sea to Jerusalem, then back to Europe after stopping in Egypt to see the pyramids and the Nile River, then through the Suez Canal (which had just opened in 1869), down through the Red Sea, and around Saudi Arabia to India.

Around present-day Singapore, they spent time in China and Japan. Everyone, especially the normal everyday people, loved him, and that made an impression on the countries he visited.

Without necessarily meaning to, Grant was promoting the United States and its increased importance on a global scale.

Then across the Pacific Ocean, they landed in San Francisco, California, in the late summer of 1879. Grant took Julia up to see Fort Vancouver, where he had been stationed without her many years earlier. Then via train (since the transcontinental railway had been in place for 10 years) across the country. Multiple parades in multiple cities later, their tour was complete.

Soon after, several books were published about Grant's global tour. Clearly, Grant was in the public eye.

If I could have asked Grant a few questions at this point in his life, I would have wanted to know:

1. Do you really think you could have stopped John Wilkes Booth from shooting the president? He probably would have shot you as well.

2. The Civil War was ruinous for the nation. Could it have been avoided? Or was that not even possible?

3. What's your secret to remaining friends with people who bitterly disagree with you, even who tried to kill you during the Civil War?

Sitting and listening to Grant tell stories would have been a treat!

They settled in New York. He purchased a brownstone townhouse in New York City and heavily invested in a firm that just so happened to be managed by a crook. You guessed it, Grant got taken to the cleaners!

Wiped out is the appropriate term. He was flat broke.

Skilled at writing, he started to write articles about the Civil War, which sold quite well. It was enough to live on, but he needed more for himself and Julia.

Then in 1884, he received the worst of news. He had throat and tongue cancer, and it was terminal. I guess smoking 20-plus cigars a day is a bad habit after all!

His friend, legendary author Mark Twain, had been prodding Grant to write his memoirs. The public was still interested in the Civil War, and Twain knew it would sell, so much so that he offered to publish it under very good terms for Julia.

Grant wrote as quickly as he could, for it was a literal race against time. The public became aware of his writing and his cancer, and they watched as well. Near the end, Grant couldn't even speak, but he could write! He kept on going.

His doctor recommended fresh air, so they left the city and stayed in a cottage in Mount McGregor, New York, which is about 118 miles straight north of New York City. From there, he continued to work on his book.

Mark Twain brought him the good news that his book was preselling very well! Finally, after years and years of trying, Grant had a nonmilitary success that was his own doing. That brought him great consolation because taking care of Julia was all-important to him.

As he often did in battles, Grant came from behind and won in the nick of time. He finished his autobiography just a few days before he died on July 23, 1885. He was 63.

His two-volume book, called *Personal Memoirs of U. S. Grant,* would become a bestseller! The royalty checks, thanks to Grant's hard work and Twain's help, were more than enough to take care of Julia.

The mayor of New York City quickly reached out with an offer of a burial place for Grant in New York City. The offer included a burial site for Julia as well, beside Grant, as that was what Grant had wanted. West Point did not allow for that.

On the day of the funeral, there were more than one million people in attendance. One of his pallbearers at his funeral was none other than his life-long friend, Simon Buckner, the Confederate general he had bested years before at Fort Donelson.

Grant's body was placed in a temporary tomb. They had bigger plans for a proper tomb, to honor Grant and the role he played in American history.

While the mausoleum was being planned and then built, Julia was busy writing her own memoirs. More than anything, writing proved to be very therapeutic. She was also the first first lady to write an autobiography.

> 66 Nations, like individuals, are punished for their transgressions. 99

– ULYSSES S. GRANT

Sadly, her book, titled *The Personal Memoirs of Julia Dent Grant (Mrs. Ulysses S. Grant),* was not published in her lifetime. No publisher's offer was good enough. I'm guessing it was too hard to compete with how well her husband's book did, and she was not about to get ripped off.

Her book was finally published in 1975!

Eventually, the massive stone mausoleum (which is a tomb where the bodies are laid to rest above ground) was ready. Built in Riverside Park on the eastern side of the Hudson River, it's the largest mausoleum in all of North America.

When Grant was "reburied" or moved to his mausoleum in 1897, more than a million people showed up for the ceremony. That's pretty amazing, considering the fact that he had been dead for more than a dozen years at that point.

People don't forget true heroes.

Five years later, in 1902, Julia died. Her final resting place is right where Grant wanted it, right beside him.

If you haven't been to Grant's Tomb, you should go. Now that you know just who is laid to rest there, you can give thanks for men like him who helped shape our country.

| **Ulysses S. Grant**
1822–1885 | | **Frederick Douglass**
1817–1895 |

Frederick Douglass advised many presidents, including Ulysses S. Grant. When Grant was president, he appointed Douglass to a special committee that worked with present-day Dominican Republic. Grant, raised by abolitionist parents, signed the 15th Amendment.

CHAPTER 14

Frederick Douglass
1817–1895

While Ulysses S. Grant was fighting to abolish slavery from the top down, there were many others who were fighting to abolish slavery from the bottom up. One of those individuals was Frederick Douglass.

Interestingly, Frederick Douglass chose the last name of "Douglass" after he escaped slavery as an adult. Prior to that, he was Frederick Bailey.

Douglass' mother was a slave in eastern Maryland on the peninsula of land that is shared with Delaware, across the Chesapeake Bay from Baltimore, Maryland. His grandmother pretty much raised him and several other children. The older slaves took care of the children so that the working-age slaves could be more productive. His mother died when he was young.

He ended up being sent over to Baltimore to live in the house of the plantation owner. Rumor was that his father was white and was one of the owners, but nobody knows for sure (and those who knew certainly weren't talking).

It was there that his life took a decisive turn. It was the 1820s, and teaching slaves to read, much less to write, was banned. Virginia (which was not much farther south and shared the southern tip of the same peninsula where he was born) and several southern states had actual laws that punished anyone who taught a slave to read or write. Laws that promised fines, floggings, or imprisonment were followed for a reason.

But Sophia Auld, the plantation owner's wife, chose to go against the norm and taught Douglass the alphabet. Her teaching was soon stopped, but he had the basics. From there, he taught himself to read. He was only 12 years old, but even then, the world was beginning to open to him.

Working wherever he was sent, Douglass also read everything he could get his hands on. Then he taught other slaves how to read and write as well.

At age 16, his life took another turn. He did it himself this time. It was a choice he made. He had been working in the tobacco fields owned by an especially cruel man who regularly beat him when Douglass decided that he had had enough.

Douglass fought back. He probably knew he could be shot, killed, or imprisoned for physically fighting with the white owner, but he didn't care. It was a lengthy bare-knuckle brawl, but it forever sealed in Douglass' heart that he was indeed a free man. Oddly, the plantation owner stopped beating Douglass after that.

> 66 Knowledge makes a man unfit to be a slave. 99
>
> – FREDERICK DOUGLASS

A few years later, Douglass tried to run away, but he was caught, beaten, and jailed. Not long after that, he tried again, and was again captured. I wonder why his owner didn't sell him or ship him off somewhere because it was just a matter of time until Douglass succeeded in escaping.

Sure enough, that happened in 1838. And this time, Douglass got away, thanks to the help of Anna Murray, a free Black woman he had met and fallen in love with while working in the Baltimore area.

She would be one of the greatest things that ever happened to him.

Anna Murray Douglass

Anna Murray was born free in Denton, Maryland, also on the eastern side of Maryland, very close to where Douglass was born. She found work as a housekeeper and laundress in Baltimore, which is where she met Douglass.

Her being free and both talking about marriage meant only one thing—he had to be free as well. Thankfully, she could help. With her own money, some ingenuity, and some falsified paperwork, she gave him what he needed to go by train through Philadelphia and on to New York City. He stayed with members of the Underground Railroad. She followed soon after.

They promptly got married and moved about 200 miles farther up the coast to New Bedford, Massachusetts. They chose the "Douglass" last name, which certainly helped protect them from anyone who might be looking for escaped slave Frederick Bailey.

In New Bedford, they both worked. He preached, taught Sunday school, and began to travel and speak about abolishing slavery. She became a shoe cobbler, in addition to her other skills, all in an effort to help provide for the growing family. They had five children together, with one dying as a child.

My guess is that she brought in more money than he did. Truly, if it wasn't for her working, Douglass would have been forced to get a steadier job that paid the bills. That, in turn, would have kept him out or at least limited his role in the abolition movement.

We owe our thanks to Anna for all she did. Years later, her daughter Rosetta wrote these words:

"The story of Frederick Douglass' hopes and aspirations and longing desire for freedom has been told—you all know it. It was a story made possible by the unswerving loyalty of Anna Murray."

She also played an active part in the abolition movement and the Underground Railroad's effort to ferry runaway slaves to free states or to Canada. Serving and helping others is what she did, and she did it her entire life.

> 66 It is easier to build strong children than to repair broken men. 99
>
> – FREDERICK DOUGLASS

In 1882, after 44 years of marriage, she died at their home, which was in Washington, D.C., at the time. In 1895, when Douglass died, she was reburied beside him in Rochester, New York's, Mount Hope Cemetery, which sits on the Genesee River that flows into Lake Ontario. Lifelong friend, Susan B. Anthony, is buried in the same cemetery.

Starting Life as a Free Man

Technically, Douglass wasn't free. He was a runaway slave, which meant he could be returned should he be discovered. Therefore, a certain level of staying under the radar was the best course of action.

But that was not for Douglass!

He was becoming more and more vocal in his abolition speeches, and the more he spoke, the more people wanted to know about him. Noted abolitionist William Garrison encouraged him to write his autobiography, which promptly became a bestseller.

That pretty much blew the lid off his plans for anonymity, so he left for England and stayed there for two years, all the while speaking out against slavery. England's Abolition Act of 1833 had outlawed the buying and owning of slaves, so I think his aim was to put pressure on America.

During all that time, Anna was back home taking care of the kids and providing for the family. She served Douglass and their family her entire life. Unfortunately, she was pretty much left behind in his rise to fame.

While in England, his supporters raised enough money to buy his freedom from the Auld family in Baltimore. Letters were written, money was paid, and paperwork was handed over. When he came home in 1847, he truly was a free man.

And then he went to work at a whole new level!

He packed up the family and moved to Rochester, New York, which is right across Lake Ontario from Canada, so they could be an active part of the Underground Railroad.

Then he started his own newspaper, *The North Star,* which pushed all the more to end slavery. Some of his children were old enough to help with the newspaper, and that gave them interests and skills they would use later in life. He ended up merging his paper with another, but for 12 years, he kept the pressure on.

The Mexican-American War came and went, but Black people were not allowed to wear the uniform. That angered Douglass, but his time on that point would come.

He also got involved in the fight for women's rights and even spoke at the Seneca Falls Convention 50 miles away in Seneca Falls, New York. It was the very first convention for women's rights in the history of the United States.

Douglass was a big supporter of women's rights, but years later, he got kickback from women's groups for supporting the 15th Amendment—which Ulysses S. Grant would approve after the Civil War— because it did not give rights to women to vote. That would not come until the 19th Amendment more than 70 years later.

The Civil War and Beyond

As the Civil War rolled across the country, every word Douglass said had more meaning. From President Abraham Lincoln, who regularly asked for Douglass's advice, to the general public, the Black people who were free as a result of the newly proclaimed Emancipation Proclamation, freemen, and the Black people who wanted to fight in the Civil War, everyone listened to what he said.

Lincoln asked Douglass to help recruit Black people into the Union army, and that was exactly what Douglass had been waiting for. He believed that fighting for freedom not only helped gain freedom for everyone else, it also brought freedom at a personal level.

Douglass traveled extensively throughout the northern states to recruit Black men to fight for the Union. The Emancipation Proclamation not only brought freedom, but it also allowed Black people to serve in the military. Two or three of his sons even joined the Union army.

Oddly enough, Douglass was nominated in 1872 for vice president on the ticket for the Equal Rights Party. He had no idea his name was even in the hat. Nothing came of it, but it showed how big his name was if they thought it might help gain votes because of him.

One thing did come of it that was not good or expected. Someone burned his Rochester, New York, home to the ground! Arson was suspected, but for which of the causes he supported would blame be assigned?

Nobody was home at the time, but the loss of personal items was significant, especially his writings.

From Rochester, he moved the family to Washington, D.C. After a few years, he moved a little farther out of the main city, across the Anacostia River but still in D.C., to a house on about 10 acres that he called "Cedar Hill." It was ideal for his family, his love of nature, and his constant writings.

Multiple presidents after Lincoln, especially Ulysses S. Grant, appointed Douglass to various committees or positions of leadership. His insight and influence were sought after.

Talk about being the right person in the right place at the right time! People listened to whatever he said, and that was a power that Douglass had.

If were able to ask him a few questions, I would like to know:

1. Today, people are calling for segregation again. What would you say about that?
2. Today, more Black babies are killed each year by abortion than are born. What would you say about that?
3. Today, the color of our skin is seen as more important than character, skill, honor, or truth. What would you say about that?

I don't think he would recognize some aspects of our country today. His voice of reason would be a welcome sound in today's virtue signaling that takes place in all levels of politics, business, education, entertainment, and media.

While working yet again on a revision of his biography, Douglass hired an editor/assistant whose name was Helen Pitts. She was an abolitionist, fought for women's rights, and believed in many of the same causes that he did. Interestingly, she happened to be a direct descendant from the Pilgrims of 1620 on the *Mayflower*.

Anna's health had been deteriorating, and in 1882, she died. She had brought the family through so much, supporting Douglass every step of the way. Their children were all grown. She had done well. She was 71 years old.

Without her, we would not have had the Frederick Douglass that we know today.

Helen Pitts Douglass

In 1884, Douglass and Helen Pitts were married and took up residence at his Cedar Hill estate. He was 67, she was 46. She had been a schoolteacher at a freedmen school in Virginia and was an editor for several women's rights organizations when they first met.

She was also white, which really upset a lot of people, including his own children.

About that, Douglass wrote:

"People who had remained silent over the unlawful relations of white slave masters with their colored slave women loudly condemned me for marrying a wife a few shades lighter than myself."

He also added:

"This proves I am impartial. My first wife was the color of my mother and the second, the color of my father."

So, the rumor was true! But I like how Douglass called it. He didn't pretend or deflect. Instead, he said it how it was. That, of course, made a lot of people upset, but for the honest and logical ones out there, he was speaking the truth.

Two women who continued to support Douglass were Elizabeth Stanton and Susan B. Anthony, both women's rights activists who worked regularly with Douglass.

Douglass had official appointments that took him to Haiti, and Helen traveled and lived with him there. They also spent several months in and around Europe. He spoke often, and she was usually with him.

In 1895, after 11 years of marriage to Helen, Frederick Douglass suddenly died. He spoke at a women's rights meeting and then went home, where he died of an apparent heart attack.

He fought for what he believed in until the very day he died. At his funeral, many people spoke, including Susan B. Anthony.

It is at this point that Helen really stepped up. The children of Douglass and Anna wanted to sell Cedar Hill. Maybe she was still seen as an outsider, I don't know, but she wanted Cedar Hill to be a memorial to Douglass for generations to come.

> 66 I am a Republican, a black, dyed in the wool Republican, and I never intend to belong to any other party than the party of freedom and progress. 99
>
> – FREDERICK DOUGLASS

She had to buy the building and the land first, so she traveled and spoke about Douglass in an effort to raise funds. The more she talked and spread the vision, the more money she raised. Eventually, she was able to buy it!

She also pressed Congress to create FDMHA, which is the Frederick Douglass Memorial and Historical Association. When she died, the house and property would go to the charity, which would then keep the place going, keep paying off the mortgage, and keep the vision of Douglass alive.

Helen died in 1903, only eight years after Douglass. She was buried in the Douglass family plot at Mouth Hope Cemetery back in Rochester, New York.

Countless individuals worked, gave money, took care of the grounds, spread the vision, and believed in the vision, all to keep the Douglass Memorial going. Finally, in 1962, President John F. Kennedy signed a law that made the Douglass Memorial estate part of the National Park System. You can visit it the next time you are in Washington, D.C.

From uneducated slave to counselor of presidents, the irony is impossible to miss. I am forever thankful for men like Frederick Douglass who tirelessly pushed toward a better America.

Frederick Douglass **Susan B. Anthony**
1817–1895   1820–1906

Frederick Douglass and Susan B. Anthony fought for each other's causes. Over the years, they shared many stages together. They were lifelong friends, much to the chagrin of many people who could not separate person from cause. She spoke at his funeral, and in death, they share the same cemetery.

CHAPTER 15

Susan B. Anthony
1820-1906

Have you ever seen one of those Susan B. Anthony dollar coins that are the size of a regular quarter but are worth a full dollar? There are differences, of course, between a coin dollar and a coin quarter, but the idea of a dollar coin never really caught on in the general public, so they pretty much disappeared from circulation.

To me, the Susan B. Anthony coin that was minted more than 70 years after her death was a uniquely fitting tribute to a woman who was a multiplier to an extreme degree. She spent her entire life fighting for a cause that she would not get to enjoy, but every woman today in the United States gets to enjoy it.

One person brought benefits to millions! That is multiplication.

What was this cause that she gave her life for? It was the right of women to vote in US elections.

Fighting for a Just Cause

Anthony was born in Adams, Massachusetts, which is the far northwest corner of the state. Her Quaker parents were outspoken in their religious beliefs and in putting an end to slavery, and little Anthony seemed well suited for what was to come.

At age three, she could read and write! I wish I had been that smart, but it was her gift and she used it wisely. Then off to a boarding school when she was older, then a Quaker seminary, and then teaching at a women-only school.

This was the 1840s in America. New states were being added to the Union, which had to decide if they would be slave states or free states. Cotton exports as a result of the cotton gin were running at all-time highs, the Mexican-American War opened up the West, and Frederick Douglass's book came out. All the while, the nation rumbled.

Also during that time, several different families were moving into position.

- Anthony, her six siblings, and her parents moved to Rochester, New York.

- Frederick and Anna Douglass and their five children also moved to Rochester.
- Elizabeth Stanton, her lawyer abolitionist husband, and their growing family (eventually seven children) moved to nearby Seneca Falls, New York.

Clearly, something was about to happen. Anthony just didn't know it at the time.

> 66 I do not assume that woman is better than man. I do assume that she has a different way of looking at things. 99
>
> – Susan B. Anthony

One thing about Anthony was that when she decided on what was right, she did something about it. She wouldn't just complain about it or wish someone else would do something about it. Not at all. She would take action herself, and her dogged determination to see that justice was served brought her attention from others.

The temperance (and abstinence) movement against alcohol was in full swing, the abolition movement was picking up speed, but it was the suffrage movement (the right of women to vote) that really captured her heart.

Soon after moving to Rochester, she met Frederick Douglass and Elizabeth Stanton. Stanton had already helped women gain more rights through her constant pressuring of Congress. She and her lawyer husband were quite the duo.

It wasn't long before she was working with Stanton, speaking, writing, and planning. They themselves were a great combo, for each had complimentary skills that benefited the cause.

Anthony was also an active member in the local abolition movement, which included numerous speakers, including Frederick Douglass. She and Douglass became lifelong friends, and she (despite the opposition of many women) spoke at his funeral.

She also became friends with and worked with Harriet Tubman of the Underground Railroad. After the Civil War, Tubman was a great promoter of women's right to vote.

Throughout the Civil War, Anthony made her voice heard for the abolition of slavery. I'm sure she rejoiced with her friend, Frederick Douglass, when the Emancipation Proclamation finally came out.

She undoubtedly was raised knowing Romans 12:15, which says, "Rejoice with those who rejoice, and weep with those who weep" (New King James Version).

There was much rejoicing, but for Anthony, there remained much yet to do.

Women's Rights After the Civil War

When the Civil War was over, Anthony and Stanton jumped full-time into fighting for the rights of women. Blacks were free and had the right to vote. Women did not. Together, they created their own equal rights association and their own women's rights newspaper.

Harriet Tubman Postage Stamp

When Black people gained the right to vote, Anthony and others pressed for women to have the same rights. They repeatedly failed, but Anthony would never take no for an answer. She pressed on. She traveled and spoke everywhere she could, even as far west as California (after the transcontinental railway was in place), always pushing for equal rights. She spoke from outside Independence Hall in Philadelphia, Pennsylvania. She even met with Queen Victoria while speaking in England, but she felt the Queen was not doing enough for women.

In 1872, she famously "crossed the line" and illegally voted in the presidential election between Ulysses S. Grant (a fellow abolitionist) and Horace Greeley. Grant of course won, but Anthony was arrested and fined $100.

Interestingly, not only did she never pay the $100 fine, but those who arrested her did not force her to pay it. My guess is that pressing the matter would have created more sympathy for her, so the powers that be just let it slide.

If you have heard the phrase, "If you want it done right, do it yourself," it was probably written about Susan B. Anthony. If she was not invited, allowed to speak, given a voice, passed over, or the message was not clear, she promptly went out and started her own organization.

She did this with the temperance movement, the abolition of slavery, women's rights, suffrage, international women's rights, and even a women's union. Her voice would be heard, no matter what.

Her belief in her cause would never die. And God help you if you stood in her way!

In addition to helping write many books with other people, and writing for her and Stanton's newspaper, she also authored her own biography.

> 66 Nothing is hopeless that is right. 99
>
> – SUSAN B. ANTHONY

I don't know how many hours in a day she worked, but my guess is that she worked probably 20 hours a day for what she believed in. She could speak, write, fundraise, plan, lecture, promote, and organize events that brought in masses of people, which meant there was never a quiet moment.

No wonder she never got married. She was married to her job, and her job was everything to her.

In the pictures I've seen of her, she is never smiling. I don't know if it was a thing at the time to not appear happy, but she never looked it. At the same time, though, I get it. She fought unwaveringly for something that she never achieved, and that is so sad.

Near the end of her life, she told a friend, "To think I have had more than 60 years of hard struggle for a little liberty, and then to die without it seems so cruel."

Indeed, that does sound cruel. So not having a smile on a photo, I'll live with that.

Eventually, by staying true to her vision and message, by sheer will and determination, and living a long time, she became something of a national celebrity. Derision turned to respect. She was applauded at national events and even at events in England and continental Europe.

> 66 I look for the day . . . when the only criterion of excellence or position shall be the ability and character of the individual; and this time will come. 99
>
> – SUSAN B. ANTHONY

But no matter where she went, she took her message. It was a constant. And she just wouldn't stop. At age 85, you would have seen her sitting down with President Teddy Roosevelt to discuss the right of women to vote.

When the 19th Amendment came before Congress in 1920, they knew it by another name, the "Susan B. Anthony Amendment." And it passed! Women finally had the right to vote.

Sadly, Anthony died in 1906 at age 86. She would miss the momentous occasion, but millions of women were there for it. And she lived through them all. That is multiplication at the highest level.

Thousands came to her funeral and passed by her casket. Anthony was buried in the Mount Hope Cemetery in her hometown of Rochester, New York. Her lifelong friend, Frederick Douglass, is buried there as well. Today, her home in Rochester, where she spent much of her life and died, is a museum and a National Historic Landmark.

The first woman to be on a US dollar coin would be an honor reserved for Susan B. Anthony, and with the minting of about 700 million one-dollar coins, the nation was reminded many, many times over just how impactful her life had been.

Oh, to make that type of impact.

Susan B. Anthony **Andrew Carnegie**
1820–1906 1835–1919

Susan B. Anthony probably rode Andrew Carnegie's trains, crossed his steel bridges, and slept in his sleeper trains while speaking across the nation about emancipation and women's rights. One friend in common was Booker T. Washington of the Tuskegee Institute. Both Anthony and Carnegie helped in their own ways to improve the lives of Black people in America. The impact they made lives on.

CHAPTER 16

Andrew Carnegie

1835–1919

In 1848, telegraph lines were beginning to crisscross the eastern states, the end of the Mexican-American War fully opened the West, and every train line was still east of the Mississippi. This meant the pent-up people in the East were about to flood into the untamed West!

The westward expansion would mean more of everything, especially trains, industry, steel, trade, farming, travel, real estate, and people. The dam was about to burst.

That same year, 13-year-old Andrew Carnegie and his family immigrated to the US from Scotland. They made their way to Pittsburgh, Pennsylvania, where they stayed with some of their relatives.

Climbing the Ladder of Success

Young Carnegie wasted no time. His dad was in the cotton industry, so Carnegie found work as a bobbin boy. That basically meant he raced around the factory, replacing full bobbins with empty ones, and taking the full bobbins to the workers who needed them. Since there was no electricity back then, he worked when the sun was up, which meant long days!

The next year, he tried for an upgrade. Instead of running around the mill, he landed a job running around town as a messenger, delivering telegraphs from the telegraph office to virtually every business, hotel, office, and person around.

Obviously, there was more money in sending a telegraph than in delivering it, so Carnegie taught himself (a secret that would work his entire life) what he needed to know. It was also a lot more comfortable to sit inside an office rather than run down the city streets through every weather variation.

Self-learning works anywhere, any time, and it doesn't matter if you have a formal education (Carnegie did not) or not. If you need to know something, figure it out. That's how you get ahead. I love that logic, and it hasn't changed from that day to this.

Before long, Carnegie was a telegraph operator, just as he planned. Then using that skill, he landed a job at age 18 in the Pennsylvania Railroad. Yes, the same Pennsylvania Railroad that is on your Monopoly game!

> 66 He that cannot reason is a fool. He that will not is a bigot. He that dare not is a slave. 99
>
> – ANDREW CARNEGIE

It was here that Carnegie happened to find two treasures. First was his boss, who actively looked for ways to help Carnegie get better, learn about the industry, make investments, understand costs and profits, manage people, etc. Perhaps it was because Scott saw the skills in Carnegie and knew any assistance would be mutually beneficial. Either way, it was a win for Carnegie.

The second treasure was unexpected. There was a businessman in town by the name of Colonel James Anderson who had fought in the War of 1812. What Anderson did that revolutionized Carnegie's world was to allow young men like Carnegie access to his personal library. It was a mini public library if you will.

For Carnegie, this was an incredible opportunity, and he took advantage of it! He read and devoured everything that interested him. This was his "high school" and "college" all rolled into one. His "PhD" from the school of hard knocks was his day job.

Within a few years, Carnegie was appointed superintendent of an entire section of the Pennsylvania Railroad. He had a good-paying job with lots of responsibility. From poor immigrant bobbin boy to a position of power, he had come a long way in a little over 10 years.

But Carnegie was just getting started!

Owning the Ladder to Success

They say that luck is what happens when preparation meets opportunity. I completely agree. Carnegie's work ethic and insatiable desire to improve himself certainly took care of the preparation part, but he was also in the right place at the right time.

He had the opportunity, and it was the railroad. Through it and his growing network of friends, he was able to make investment after investment in businesses and entire industries that were at the ground floor of their own rise to success.

His boss told him that 10 shares in a profitable shipping company would soon be available. Apparently, someone was selling, and if Carnegie could buy, it could be a good move. Carnegie probably had the money to buy the stock himself, but he convinced his mother to mortgage her home to buy the shares, which she did. His father had recently died, so creating a steady source of income for her and the family was a big need. He hoped the investment would prove profitable, and it did.

Carnegie had also hired his younger brother, Tom, to be his assistant and telegrapher, the same position he had held just a few years earlier. Tom was his only living sibling. Their sister died in infancy.

> 66 You cannot push any one up a ladder unless he be willing to climb a little himself. 99
>
> – Andrew Carnegie

Being able to think outside the box, to be entrepreneurial, is not only a mindset, but also an attitude. Other people see it by what you say, how you act, and what you do. It draws like-minded people to you like a magnet.

One example of that was Theodore Woodruff, an established wagon maker, who wanted to build a sleeper car for the train system. Carnegie not only supported the idea, he invested in Woodruff's company. That would prove to be a good move, as sleeper cars soon became an important railway addition. The greater the distance a train traveled, the greater the need for sleeper cars.

Years later, George Pullman and Carnegie took the sleeping car proposal to United Pacific Railroad general manager T. C. Durant, who loved it and bought in.

Carnegie also invested in oil and coal. Not only were they an emerging market, but shipping oil and coal via train was the only way to get it where it needed to go. His investments proved to be so profitable that it allowed him to invest even more into other enterprises.

He saved and reinvested. He didn't flaunt his wealth. He quietly took his profits and planted them back in the ground.

Trains run on steel tracks, and with track lines expanding across the nation and about to explode into the West, Carnegie dug deeper into iron. He studied. He went to the source. He traveled to England and learned the necessary parts of a steel plant. Then he returned and set up shop . . . his *own* shop.

In 1865, Carnegie got off the train. Literally, he quit his train job so that he could chase his passion of steel. The US market was expanding, and he intended to capture the market.

He would go on to create the world's largest steel manufacturing company. In the world! That's pretty amazing since the US came so late to the game, but it's also a testament to both Carnegie's vision as well as the country's growth potential. The nation was bursting at the seams, and Carnegie was helping meet the ever-increasing demand for steel.

But here is where his genius took things to the next level. He not only created what customers needed, such as the steel girders in a bridge, but he also had his hands in (if not complete ownership) the mining of the iron ore, the steel processing plants, and the transportation (ships and trains) to and from.

He figured out how to make money every step of the way. Simply brilliant! That is a mindset worth applying.

And then he actively looked for ways to make the process better, faster, more profitable, safer, cleaner, more efficient, etc. Always reading, he learned all he could, and if someone knew more, he'd hire them.

Like Benjamin Franklin, Carnegie was good with his tongue. He was smart, well-read, and socially aware. They didn't have golf back then, so he networked at social gatherings. He was also very good at thanking and honoring his friends, such as giving them stock or naming companies after them.

The massive entity he created would eventually be called the Carnegie Steel Company. It was the main provider of steel across the country.

Then, in 1901 at the age of 65, he sold out to the legendary financier and investment banker, J. P. Morgan, for $480 million. That would equate, some say, to more than $300 billion today! Either way, that is a ton of money.

Giving It All Away

Carnegie not only read a lot, he also wrote a lot. In his articles and books were several themes or life principles, including:

- No man becomes rich unless he enriches others.
- The man who dies rich, dies disgraced.
- Do real and permanent good in this world.

He was well-known, and tens of thousands of people, if not millions, had read what he wrote. The question I'm sure they wanted to ask was whether he would live by his own words or not.

Thankfully, and thankfully for us as a nation, Carnegie was a man of his word.

> " A library outranks any other one thing a community can do to benefit its people. It is a never-failing spring in the desert. "
>
> – ANDREW CARNEGIE

When Carnegie sold his Carnegie Steel Company, some say he was at that moment the richest man in the world. Who knows if that was the case or not.

His younger brother, Tom, had done well himself. Thanks to big brother's advice and help, Tom made millions. So much so that he created a massive sprawling estate on Cumberland Island, which sits just off the coast of Georgia. He purchased it from the descendants of Nathaniel and Catherine Greene. This was the same Catherine Greene who helped fund Eli Whitney and his early cotton gin models. When she died in 1814, she was buried there on Cumberland Island.

Tom and his wife, Lucy, had nine children. They enjoyed the estate on Cumberland Island and would spend about six months there each year.

Tragically, Tom died only a couple years after his estate was built. His wealth then went to his wife and children, with the children each receiving millions of dollars. Some of their descendants still live on the estate on the island.

Also sad is the fact that some of these awe-inspiring buildings from Tom's estate are nothing but fallen-down structures that are open to the elements. To me, it's such a depressing ending to what was once palatial living where the rich wined and dined and the famous got married.

Interestingly, Carnegie himself did not get married until after his brother and mother had both died. Margaret Carnegie died within a month of Tom dying (of pneumonia). The next year (1887), Carnegie married Louise Whitfield.

Carnegie and Louise had met seven years earlier, when he was 45 years old and she was 23. They were first good friends, and then as the relationship deepened, he proposed, but Carnegie's mother would not have it. So, Carnegie put the marriage on hold, though secretly he and Louise remained close friends. When Margaret died, they set a marriage date.

For the next 32 years, the two were inseparable. Carnegie valued his wife's input and advice. She was his confidant, and he needed one with the direction his life was taking. Within four years, he would be retired and sitting on one of the biggest fortunes of all time.

They had only one child, Margaret, who came in 1897.

During Carnegie's retirement years, from when he sold his company (1901) until he died (1919), he and Louise were busy giving away his millions. They traveled a lot as a family, while making the rounds between their three places: their house in New York City, their summer house in Lenox, Massachusetts, and his Skibo Castle in Scotland.

66 Man must have no idol and the amassing of wealth is one of the worst species of idolatry! No idol is more debasing than the worship of money! 99

– ANDREW CARNEGIE

Together, they would administer his $480 million to the world.

No doubt they were accosted on every side by people, causes, institutions, and organizations that wanted his money. "Where do we begin?" must have been one of the questions they asked themselves.

For Carnegie, one of his loves was the idea of gifting public libraries to cities so that those who wanted to better themselves could do so, just as he had done when he was a teen.

About that, he wrote,

"It was from my own early experience that I decided there was no use to which money could be applied so productive of good to boys and girls who have good within them and ability and ambition to develop it, as the founding of a public library in a community."

So that's what he did, but on a grand scale! (Of course, everything Carnegie did was on a grand scale.) Almost 3,000 libraries came as a result, with most of those across the US. Do a little research online and you may find your public library is one that came to be as a result of Carnegie's generosity.

After libraries, he chose to put a lot of money into education. Sometimes it was on a personal level, such as traveling to Tuskegee, Alabama, and donating substantially to Booker T. Washington and the Tuskegee Institute (now Tuskegee University) or funding various educational causes in his birth town back in Scotland.

Sometimes it was more distant through the founding of trusts and foundations that would continue to provide for educational needs across America and in Canada, England, Scotland, and beyond. With all the foundations and trusts that Carnegie created, each with its own independent board of trustees, I wouldn't be surprised if nobody knows the true number of schools or people that have benefited from his initial financial gifts.

Believe it or not, the long-lasting children's TV show, *Sesame Street*, was created with Carnegie's foundation money. A lot of people benefited from that show, and still do (if you subtract out all the PC, woke garbage), since it began back in 1969.

What's amazing is that his trusts and foundations still churn out the money, more than 100 years since he founded them! That is incredible and a true testament to investing in the future.

Oddly enough, he loved pipe organs (and Scottish bagpipes!) and provided more than 7,500 organs to churches across the US and around the world. As for bagpipes, the Carnegie Mellon University (which Carnegie founded) is the only university in the US that offers a bagpipe major. Carnegie sure loved his bagpipes!

Both libraries and education touched upon the premise of providing help to people who would use that assistance to better themselves in some way. It's that proverbial difference between giving a man a fish (good for the day) or teaching a man how to fish (good for a lifetime).

In his famous "The Gospel of Wealth" article on money, he wrote some of the best thoughts on charity that I have ever read. Consider his words carefully:

"In bestowing charity, the main consideration should be to help those who will help themselves; to provide part of the means by which those who desire to improve may do so; to give those who desire to use the aids by which they may rise; to assist, but rarely or never to do all. Neither the individual nor the race is improved by alms-giving."

During all this time, Carnegie's practical mind came to want something else—world peace. I mean, after all, it only makes logical sense. Every problem has an answer. Why not work it out rather than kill each other?

So he created the Peace Palace in The Hague, Netherlands, as a place where countries could come to work out their differences. His foundation still owns and manages it to this day and there is a permanent court of arbitration. What an incredible dream!

Through his peace efforts, he tried desperately to help convince Germany not to go to war. Minds were not convinced, however, and World War I erupted. It would be the bloodiest war of all time, a fact that I think Carnegie envisioned due to the advances and limits of technology. The war would finally end in 1919, just a couple months before Carnegie died.

Carnegie was known for saying,

"The thoughtful man must shortly say, 'I would as soon leave to my son a curse as the almighty dollar.'"

Those were serious words, but he did just that. He provided for Louise and Margaret, but not to the tune of millions and millions, which he could easily have done.

Like his brother, Carnegie died of pneumonia. He was 83 years old, almost twice as old as younger brother Tom when he died.

Carnegie died at his Lenox, Massachusetts, summer home and was buried in Sleepy Hollow Cemetery in Sleepy Hollow, New York. Besides a few family members of the Astor and Rockefeller families, the cemetery also holds Washington Irving, who wrote *The Legend of Sleepy Hollow* and *Rip Van Winkle*. Sleepy Hollow is just 30 miles north of New York City on the Hudson River.

If I could have grabbed Carnegie for a few minutes, I would have asked him:

1. World peace . . . war isn't always logical, but doesn't the fact that it's illogical also make it pretty much impossible to mediate?

2. Giving to those who help themselves . . . I love that, but what do you do with needy people who don't actually want to help themselves at all?

3. Giving to our children . . . it's natural that we want to pass our wealth on to our children, but when does it

become a curse rather than a blessing? Where do we draw that line?

After Carnegie died, the millions he had not yet given away went directly into his foundations. Louise continued the vision and philanthropy work that they had been doing together for the rest of her life. If you have ever been to Carnegie Hall, you have Louise to thank. She died in 1946 at age 89.

> 66 I am the unknown wife of a somewhat well-known businessman. 99

> – LOUISE CARNEGIE

Margaret grew up, got married just a few months before Carnegie died, had four children, and played a part in the family foundations until she died in 1990. She was 93.

All three are buried in Sleepy Hollow Cemetery.

With all that money, it was never about glitz and glamor. It was not a walk of pride, showing the world how rich, good, smart, or above everyone else he was. Not at all. Carnegie said, believed, and acted upon the following:

"Wealth is not to feed our egos, but to feed the hungry and to help people help themselves."

This truth applies to all of us. So let's do just that.

Andrew Carnegie
1835–1919

★

George Washington Carver
1864–1943

Both Andrew Carnegie and George Washington Carver were friends of Booker T. Washington and believed in the Tuskegee Institute. When Carnegie visited Tuskegee, Carver was already teaching there. Carnegie gave a sizeable donation to Tuskegee, while Carver gave his entire life savings (upon his death).

CHAPTER 17

George Washington Carver

1864-1943

Thanks to Eli Whitney and the cotton gin, farmers in the southern states went crazy with cotton, which promptly became the top US export and stayed that way for decades. Business was booming!

All that planting and replanting of cotton eventually depleted the soil. The cotton yield was continually decreasing and a new crop was needed. That, combined with the Civil War being over and freed slaves, the South was in desperate need of something besides cotton.

Farmers in the South, whether they farmed on a few acres or a few thousand acres, needed real answers that they could take to the bank. They didn't need fake answers, PC answers, political-party answers, or anything that gave money to anyone other than the farmer putting food on the table.

Did such answers exist? Who could help?

Thankfully, help was coming. His name was George Washington Carver, and he was the right man at the right time with the right skills, and with the right heart.

But he almost never made it. From birth, it seemed that the odds were stacked against him. Carver was born in 1864, after the Emancipation Proclamation but before the Civil War was over, on a farm in southwestern Missouri.

Missouri was a slave state, though not located in the South. It was first populated by Northerners and then by Southerners. Similarly, the governors at that time were pro-Union and then pro-Confederate. Soldiers came from both sides during the Civil War. Clearly, it was a state going through a lot of changes.

The farm (near Diamond, Missouri, which is still a farming community) where his slave mother worked was owned by Moses Carver, a white farmer who was opposed to slavery. While still a baby and while the state was in flux, he was kidnapped. His mother, sister, and he, probably along with a bunch of other freed slaves in the surrounding areas, were taken east to Kentucky to be sold back into slavery. Somehow, they missed his older brother, and his father was already dead.

This type of marauding activity was common during the Civil War. It was a quick way to make a buck for scoundrels who, just like today, make money off other people.

Moses couldn't leave his farm, so he paid a neighbor to try to find them. Sadly, all he was able to find was baby Carver. His mother and sister were sold and gone, never to be seen again. Carver was brought back, and he and his older brother were basically adopted by the Carvers.

Moses' wife, Susan, taught the boys to read and write. Young Carver was often sick, and he was skinny, so he was inside more. Susan decided to teach him everything she knew. It was the original Home Economics class, one that we all should have received growing up!

Carver was especially interested in all things plants. He got so good with plants, whether gardens or crops or orchards, that even at a young age he helped nearby farmers with problems they faced.

He probably learned everything he could from the Carvers, for they sent him to a new all-Black school in Neosho, Missouri, which was just 11 miles south. He stayed with the Watkins family (he got free room and board in exchange for his home ec skills) while going to school.

> 66 Where there is no vision, there is no hope. 99

> – George Washington Carver

Mrs. Watkins was a midwife who most likely delivered every baby in and around Neosho for several generations. One of the babies she delivered was Thomas Hart Benton, who became a world-famous painter. He was born in 1889, almost 20 years after Carver lived in Neosho, and he died in 1975.

She made a deep impact on Carver in two ways: her secrets of herbal medicine and her Christian faith. Apparently, she gave him a Bible that he kept and read for years and years afterward. They kept in touch, even after he became famous. She died in 1925 at age 101.

Within a couple years, Carver had maxed out the Neosho school as well, so he decided to move on. He was only 13 years old, but he launched out on his own, using his skills to pay the bills. He moved around, went to various schools, and graduated from a high school in the middle of Kansas.

He applied to a college, was accepted, and then rejected as soon as they found out he wasn't white. A few years later, he applied again, this time to a school that took anyone who qualified. There he studied art and music, but his professor recommended that Carver study what he was most passionate about—plants.

Thankfully, Carver followed that advice. He was accepted into an agriculture college, today's Iowa State University, where he completed both his bachelor's and master's degrees.

It was 1896, and Carver was ready to step onto the world's stage. At 32, he was a little older than most college graduates, but the obstacles he faced that slowed him up would have stopped most people. Carver was relentless and persevering, character traits that would serve him well.

Booker T. Washington, the first principal and chief fundraiser for the Tuskegee Institute down in Tuskegee, Alabama, recruited Carver to lead their agriculture school. There was one perk that Carver received (besides higher pay) that apparently irked the other professors at Tuskegee. Carver was given two rooms, one for himself and one for his plants!

But Tuskegee Institute would be his home, his life, and his base of operations for everything that was to come. I firmly believe that Tuskegee got an amazing deal with Carver! The entire nation benefited from Carver.

Seeing the Need

Carver was finally in the deep South. He was in the middle of southern farms that had been home to King Cotton. I bet that by the time his train stopped in Tuskegee, Alabama, Carver was already aware of many of the challenges that local farmers faced.

The soil was beyond depleted. Erosion was everywhere. Crop yield was way down. Quite simply, it was a mess!

It's hard to imagine, but from the moment Eli Whitney's cotton gin was introduced until that moment, cotton was seen as the only crop worth planting. And Whitney had introduced the cotton gin back in 1794! Carver arrived in 1896.

That means that for more than 100 years, the soil had known nothing else, and it was virtually dead.

As a natural result, farmers were poor, especially Black farmers. Yes, they were free, but they often worked land they didn't own and had to share a portion of the yield, thus the term "sharecropping." With cotton crops producing less and less each season, it seemed like a dead-end life for many—and it really was.

Amazingly, Carver had real answers.

At Tuskegee, Carver was both teacher as well as researcher, chemist, tester, and trainer in the community. Way more than enough work for one person, but Carver often worked 16-hour days!

First, he had to diagnose the problem, then he had to come up with answers, and then he had to take (sell) his ideas to the public.

Problem: soil severely depleted, uneducated farmers, poor farmers, and inefficient farming

Answers: different crops (such as peanuts, sweet potatoes, soybeans, certain nut trees), crop rotation, crops that add nutrients to the soil, and soil fertilization

Training the public: handouts, brochures, and a show-and-tell wagon, drawn by two mules, packed with samples, tools, and teaching materials, from which Carver could train hundreds of farmers each month

Unbeknownst to Carver, another challenge would soon develop. When people did what he suggested (because it worked) and started growing different crops besides cotton, they would need a market that would buy what they produced.

Creating practical uses: Carver developed hundreds of uses for what was grown, especially with peanuts and sweet potatoes.

> 66 It is not the style of clothes one wears, neither the kind of automobile one drives, nor the amount of money one has in the bank that counts. These mean nothing. It is simply service that measures success. 99
>
> – George Washington Carver

The soil was the biggest problem, and Carver knew that it would take years to remedy. It was not a quick fix, nor could it be an expensive one. Few Black farmers in the south could afford store-bought fertilizers for their fields, and since they were usually leasing the land anyway, there seemed to be no reason for it.

Things were bad, and it was only going to get worse.

But if the soil could be fixed, it would bring increase to whatever crop was in the ground, including cotton. His belief was that "anything that helps fill the dinner pail is valuable." How true!

Carver set to work, applying his experience and knowledge, taking samples, testing the soils, experimenting, rotating, composting, gardening, and so much more, all with his workaholic habits. No wonder he never got married. He didn't have time for it! He literally gave his life to his work.

Meeting the Need

The big-picture goal was to help farmers move from barely surviving to thriving. Could it be done? Carver believed it was entirely possible.

It wasn't long before Carver had a plan. It involved planting crops that naturally added nitrogen back into the soil. Peanuts were the best, but sweet potatoes, soybeans, and black-eyed peas were also good for the soil. Simply planting these crops helped heal the soil.

By rotating crops, such as cotton and then peanuts and then back to cotton, the nitrogen-enriched soil not only produced a better and better cotton yield, but the additional crops also provided food for the farmers that could be eaten or sold.

Add to that homemade fertilizers that were natural and therefore cheap (or free), and local farmers had the beginnings of a farming system that could positively impact all the southern states that had relied on cotton for more than 100 years. It meant farmers on even small plots of land, especially sharecroppers, had a much better chance of success.

The best way to teach some things is to show, and that is what Carver did. He made a drawing of a traveling wagon that he wanted, and Booker T. Washington found someone to pay for it. That someone was banker and philanthropist, Morris Ketchum Jesup, who sadly died two years later. He was buried in Green-Wood Cemetery in Brooklyn, New York, the same cemetery where Samuel Morse was buried.

The wagon was built, outfitted with two mules, and off Carver went in his new Jesup Agricultural Wagon. It was 1906, the same year that Andrew Carnegie visited Tuskegee and made a big donation to the Tuskegee Institute.

Carver taught thousands of local farmers from his wagon. He always said that education was the "key to unlock the golden door of freedom," and that's exactly what he did. He took it on the road and met people right where they were. That is humility in action if I've ever seen it!

Helping people help themselves. That is the "teaching others to fish" metaphor in action. I love what he said about this with his perspective on life:

"No individual has any right to come into the world and go out of it without leaving behind him distinct and legitimate reasons for having passed through it."

So true! But he also knew reality. People won't usually change unless there is a good reason for it. If it ain't broke, don't fix it. But the agriculture system was broken! With all of that, he was fighting a statistic that he himself explained:

"Ninety-nine percent of the failures come from people who have the habit of making excuses."

Doing one thing for more than 100 years has a way of driving the habits deep! But if southern farmers were to survive, they had to diversify their crops. The soil demanded it and the economy demanded it. What's more, the boll weevil (which is virtually exclusively a killer of cotton) had come across the southern border several years earlier and was destroying the ever-shrinking cotton crops.

Farmers learned from Carver how rotating crops, diversifying crops, and feeding the soil would help them survive, stay on the land, pay their bills, and hopefully thrive. And if there was any question after that, the boll weevil removed all doubt!

Asking for God's Help

More and more people began to do as Carver instructed. They rotated, diversified, and planted crops that fed the soil. One crop led the way. It was peanuts.

And as peanut production increased, another need became apparent. People didn't know what to do with all the peanuts. There was a limit to how many someone could eat. The whole plant was good feed for the animals, but there needed to be a sufficient market for peanuts to drive the economy.

That's a lot of pressure on Carver! He had started it, so he had better give them answers.

So, Carver took it to God. That was his habit. He would get up at 4 a.m. and go for a walk and talk to God, telling God about his situation and asking God for answers to whatever he was working on.

Years later, he described what happened like this:

"I said to God, 'God, tell me the mystery of the universe.' But God answered, 'That knowledge is for me alone.' So I said, 'God, tell me the mystery of the peanut.' Then God said, 'Well George, that's more nearly your size.' And he told me."

Specifically, Carver said God told him to "separate the peanut into water, fats, oils, gums, resins, sugars, starches, and amino acids. Then recombine these under My three laws of compatibility, temperature, and pressure."

> 66 I ask Him daily and often momently to give me wisdom, understanding, and bodily strength to do His will; hence I am asking and receiving all the time. 99
>
> – GEORGE WASHINGTON CARVER

Carver acted. It was always about action with him. He never stopped moving. But he had learned the most profitable approach was to mix his actions with God's advice. It always produced better results. Sometimes he would even find answers in his sleep. He explained:

"I would often go to sleep with an apparently insoluble problem. When I woke the answer was there. Why, then, should we who believe in Christ be so surprised at what God can do with a willing man in a laboratory? Some things must be baffling to the critic who has never been born again."

Results in his research lab at Tuskegee for the practical, useful, and profitable uses of peanuts (and then sweet potatoes) began to pour out.

In addition to the long existent peanut butter and the more recent peanut oil, Carver's experiments came up with some amazing uses for peanuts that directly boosted the peanut economy.

His uses were dispersed into the community and the nation and then the world through his little handouts or brochures. He listed close to 300 different uses and recipes for the lowly peanut. It blew people away!

About asking God for help and receiving answers, Carver humbly stated,

"The Lord always provides me with life changing ideas. Not that I am special. The Lord provides everyone with life changing ideas. These ideas are quite literally a treasure from the Almighty. It is up to each of us however, to choose and dig for the treasure."

You don't hear that advice very often these days, especially from the scientific community. But why not? The Creator of the peanut certainly had good advice for the student of the peanut.

But the proof is in the pudding. Peanut production jumped and the market expanded. It was economically viable! Sweet potatoes were also a good product to consume and sell, as were the many other crops that Carver recommended using.

All of it, every step and every crop, was bringing freedom and life to everyone in the South. That was truly Carver's hope and intention, and he lived to see it come to pass.

> 66 There is no short cut to achievement. Life requires thorough preparation—veneer isn't worth anything. 99

> – GEORGE WASHINGTON CARVER

Interestingly, because he did exactly as he said (which was, "When you can do the common things of life in an uncommon way, you will command the attention of the world."), the likes of Thomas Edison, Henry Ford (who became a close friend), US presidents, and the US government came knocking on his door. So did Mahatma Gandhi, and even Joseph Stalin!

Carver chose humility and let his example do most of the talking for him. That is one trait I wish we had more of these days!

It wasn't long before the peanut crop alone was cranking out hundreds of millions of dollars each year!

Tuskegee Institute honored Carver with his own museum, the George Washington Carver Museum. It was dedicated in early 1941 by Henry Ford, along with his wife, Clara.

If I could have knocked on his laboratory door and perhaps been allowed to ask him questions while he was working, I would have asked him:

1. The entire nation knows you and respects you. What is your secret to staying humble?

2. If others wanted to be like you, what advice would you give them?

3. With all the inventions and ideas still inside of you, how many more years do you need to live to see them all to fruition?

In 1943, at age 79, Carver died and was buried at Tuskegee, right beside Booker T. Washington. Carver had added "Washington" as his middle name soon after Booker T. Washington died (back in 1915), probably as a sign of appreciation or respect.

Not only did Carver boost the agricultural economy in the South, but he also boosted the Tuskegee name. Everyone heard it mentioned, over and over. Talk about branding! What's more, Carver left his entire life's savings to Tuskegee.

The next time you drive by Diamond, Missouri, be sure to stop in and see the national monument (the first to a Black American) erected by President Franklin D. Roosevelt in Carver's honor.

We all serve mankind in some way. Do your part and don't stop until you accomplish it. As Carver used to say,

"How far you go in life depends on your being tender with the young, compassionate with the aged, sympathetic with the striving and tolerant of the weak and strong. Because someday in your life you will have been all of these."

Well said.

George Washington Carver
1864–1943

Henry Ford
1863–1947

George Washington Carver and Henry Ford were friends for many years. Ford even paid to have an elevator installed in Carver's building on the Tuskegee Institute campus so that Carver could get around more easily. The George Washington Carver School in Bryan County, Georgia, was built by Ford and dedicated in 1940. They also worked together to find alternative rubber sources during World War II.

CHAPTER 18

Henry Ford

1863-1947

With war, there are always shortages. When WWII started, one of the main concerns was rubber with its countless uses, especially the obvious wheels for vehicles and planes. At that time, almost all raw rubber came from Indonesia, and one of the first things Japan did was take control of those areas.

America was in trouble. Scientists, chemists, farmers, and inventors were tasked with coming up with a solution. Among many others, Henry Ford and George Washington Carver, who had been friends for many years, were called in.

Both in their 70s at this point, Ford and Carver could apply decades of experience to try to find a solution. Carver set up a lab near Ford in Dearborn, Michigan. Countless crops and experiments later, they found the weed goldenrod could be used to make rubber.

During that time, Ford even produced a car with its body made from soybeans rather than metal! Why that didn't take off, I don't know, unless it was simply too expensive to mass produce. One good thing is that soybeans don't rust. He was decades ahead of the stainless-steel DeLorean!

Sadly, Carver died within a year (in 1943), as did Ford's only son, Edsel Ford, who was mass producing B-24s for the US military. The Ford-Carver rubber project continued on, but in the end, someone else developed a synthetic rubber that met America's war effort needs. Never again would America be dependent on raw rubber from overseas, so gaining that freedom was a very important step.

Ford and Carver each played a part in America's pursuit of freedom, which was precisely what they had both spent their entire lives doing. Freedom is a reality for many, but only a dream for some, and that dream is always worth fighting for.

Inquisitive Minds Always Want to Know

Henry Ford was born a few months after Abraham Lincoln signed the Emancipation Proclamation in today's urban sprawl of Detroit, Michigan, right across the Detroit River from Canada. Detroit was a very busy city with the Underground Railroad in the years leading up to the Emancipation Proclamation and the Civil War.

Ford's family were farmers, so being familiar with farm machinery, crops, and the ever-present need for efficiency and profitability were no doubt very normal.

Interestingly, Ford had a penchant for taking apart watches. Eli Whitney, the inventor of the cotton gin (who died in 1825), did as well. And like Whitney, Ford could actually put them back together again.

But when young Ford saw a steam engine, he was awestruck. His mind spun with possibilities! Life on a farm could benefit in countless ways with steam engines, but there was so much more that could be done with engines!

Engines became his driving passion. At age 15, he built his own little one-cylinder engine! Someday, he even wanted to create something that he could drive without a horse. How cool is that?

The next year (1879), as Ulysses S. Grant was finishing up his two-and-a-half-year celebration tour around the world, Ford left the family farm and moved a few miles east to the big city of Detroit. He may have only been 16 years old, but he had a very specific plan. He was going to learn everything there was to know about engines.

66 Quality means doing it right when no one is looking. 99

– HENRY FORD

He worked as a mechanic. He worked at Thomas Edison's electricity company that powered a good portion of Detroit's homes using steam engines. He studied electricity. He got so good that he could diagnose and repair steam engines. And he was still a teen!

Steam engines were at their peak at this time. They were cutting edge technology. From trains to boats to farm equipment to even tractors, the steam engine made work easier and faster.

It was as if the car was just waiting to be developed and mass produced.

With most of society being agriculture based, cities were not all that populated, but as America shifted into more of an industrial age, cities would soon fill up with people. And transportation in the form of a car would become a necessity.

The need for cars was increasing by the day.

After a few years in Detroit, he returned to the farm. On the side, he still fixed steam engines. All the while, he kept tinkering and dreaming. It was just a matter of time.

At age 25, he married a neighbor and friend, Clara Bryant. She would be his lifelong bride, partner through thick and thin, and constant source of encouragement. She would outlive him by a few years. They would have one child together, Edsel Ford, who would have four children of his own.

Ford worked at a sawmill for a while, then went back to work for Thomas Edison's company and quickly rose through ranks. He befriended Edison soon after, and the two inventors would remain friends and accomplish a lot over the next few decades together.

I can't imagine rubbing shoulders and tossing ideas around with the people Ford talked with or worked with on a regular basis. That would have been absolutely incredible!

A Car for the Common Man

In 1896, the very year that George Washington Carver finished college and went to teach at Tuskegee Institute, Ford created his first car. Well, it was more of a buggy-like carriage thing with four skinny bicycle wheels and a little gas-powered engine, but it worked. Ford could drive without a horse!

As great as his little "quadricycle" was, as he called it, it was only a prototype. He wanted more. So he kept improving, always making it better. He believed the best market was the business sector, creating vehicles to deliver products or produce. That's pretty much what a train does, so producing a vehicle that would do the same for most every business in town seemed like a smart move, and indeed it was—for the most part.

With several investors, he created the Detroit Automobile Company to meet that need, but he was a pioneer in an industry that didn't even exist yet. There were no OEM (original equipment manufacturer) parts anywhere, on the planet! Think about that for a minute.

His business faltered and went bankrupt within two years. It was a failure.

He then founded the Henry Ford Company, and that didn't work out so well either. Then the investors pretty much kicked him out.

Back to the drawing board, trying all the harder to apply this truth, in Ford's own words,

"Failure is simply an opportunity to begin again; this time more intelligently."

Thankfully, Ford also had Clara in his back corner. She believed in him and encouraged him to keep on trying. Years later, Ford said about Clara, "I attribute whatever I may have been able to accomplish in life far more to my wife than to anything else and to everything else put together." That's pretty high praise, but without her, he probably would have never made it.

66 Vision without execution is just hallucination. 99

– Henry Ford

After his second failure, Ford revised his vision. He decided, most importantly, that he wanted a car that would be bought by everyone. It would be for the masses, and it would be inexpensive enough so that they could afford it.

Ford Motor Company was born in 1903, and he hoped it was "more intelligent" than the last two attempts.

Not only did Ford try to learn from his own mistakes, but he applied the successes and failures of others. Recent inventors like Eli Whitney and Samuel Colt had used interchangeable parts with great success, so he would do the same. He would eventually take Andrew Carnegie's approach of owning every step of the process to a whole new level.

What's more, Ford created an assembly line process in his factory buildings that exponentially sped up the creation time for each car. He tweaked, he improved, he built his own parts, and he kept innovating.

His Model T cars were soon rolling out, and the masses loved them! His car assembly line using interchangeable parts could produce multiple cars in a single day. It wasn't long before his factories were running 24 hours a day to try to keep up with the growing demand.

But they couldn't, even with all his streamlining and efficient practices. Another factory was needed. Ford was soon producing hundreds of thousands of cars per year and that number continued to rise.

As demand for his cars went up, Ford actually decreased the price per car. He could do so because they were making so many cars, but it was also a smart move. He gained more customers, but also showed the world that he wasn't milking his customers for all they were worth. Something to think about in our own respective worlds.

> **❝** Impossible means that you haven't found a solution yet. **❞**
>
> – HENRY FORD

Something else was happening that Ford may not have realized. Who could have? By making a car for the common man, he was making cars "normal," and if something is normal, then it's a necessity. And if it's a necessity, then it's soon expected.

This mindset shift took place on a national and global scale. Ford was of course not the only car manufacturer out there, but his Model T was the top seller and it played a huge role in the mental shift of cars moving from "oddity" to "necessity."

Believe it or not, in a period of less than 20 years, his factories cranked out more than 16,000,000 Model T cars! That is an insane number. Breaking it down shows just how mind-boggling it truly is:

- with 16,000,000-plus in 20 years,
- that's 800,000 cars a year,
- that's 2,191 cars a day,
- that's 91 cars an hour 24 hours a day,
- and that's 1.5 cars per minute!

Like I said, that's an insane number.

Only a few people on Earth would have thought of doing such a thing, but logistically being able to pull it off is a completely different thing.

For example, how do you maintain the staggering number of orders while simultaneously dealing with limitations on raw materials due to WWI, the fact that few companies can even supply the necessary parts, and the costs that might increase for whatever the reason? Not for the faint of heart!

Like a precision instrument, Ford created a precision company, the first of its kind in the world.

A Company for the World

Imagine you own a busy donut shop in a good location. Over time, you know approximately how many customers you will have every day and how many donuts you'll sell. Then, suddenly, busloads of people start lining up for your fresh donuts every single morning!

You consider stockpiling your ingredients, but bags and bags of flour sitting in your storage facility is just a money drain. And eggs, those can't be stored for too long, and the price keeps going up. As for sugar, it's getting harder to buy the amount you need because sugar plantations sell to everyone. On top of it all, shipping is hit or miss.

That's a tough situation! You never know if you'll be able to meet demand or not, if you'll make a profit or not, or if your competitor is driving you out of business or not.

Ford had an answer to this challenge:

1. Own it.
2. Stagger it.
3. Fine-tune it.

Using your donut shop as the example, here is what you do. You buy or lease the farmland that produces the wheat you need, including all the farm equipment to plant, water, and harvest your crops. You build a mill to store, grind, and bag all your flour. And you buy a convoy of trucks to bring the flour to your shop each morning.

You do this with each ingredient, such as sugar, eggs, nuts, spices, etc. You also do this for the paper boxes, napkins, plastic silverware, etc. that are part of each donut order.

Every single piece of every single thing you need, you own.

> 66 A poor man is not the one without a cent. A poor man is the one without a dream. 99
>
> – HENRY FORD

Then you stagger out exactly how much of each ingredient or product you need per day to meet demand. Maybe that's 1,000 pounds of flour. You don't bring in 900 or 1,100 pounds, just 1,000 pounds exactly at the same time every morning. You repeat this precise delivery amount with everything you use each day.

Then you fine-tune your operation so that everything in the proper amounts is on hand every morning, your crew do their specific jobs, no money or time is wasted at any point, and the whole process is efficient, seamless, and fast. What's more, you create your own power plant so you never run out of electricity for your store.

Then on top of it all, you install a drive-through window and lower your donut price! Boom! And business inevitably speeds up all the more due to your ever-increasing market share.

All of this and more, Ford did with his massive factory in Dearborn, Michigan. He had iron ore delivered by his own ships from his own mines. He had wood delivered from his own forests cut at his own mill and delivered by his own trucks. Every glass, wood, rubber, plastic, or metal part or piece, he controlled its production and delivery.

From the ground to the car showroom, he was in control. There would be no shortages or delays if he could help it.

Imagine that!

Ford's son, Edsel, had been watching and learning. He worked in various positions within the company, and in 1919, Edsel became company president. He was only 26 years old at the time. Ford still ran the show, but Edsel was at the top.

Edsel pushed for better, faster, different, and more stylish cars. Ford was not so willing to change, but he begrudgingly did at several points along the way.

When WWII came along, Edsel played a key role in mass producing bombers at the Ford factory for the US military. Any company that could help during the war was asked to help, and Edsel was more than willing to do so. Thanks to the incredible system in place, built solely by the private sector, the Ford company was able to be of significant value in WWII.

Edsel died in the middle of the war (in 1943) at the young age of 49 from stomach cancer. Ford stepped back into the president role, but soon gave that to his grandson, Henry Ford II, who remained company president until 1960.

The company continued to produce more cars and different models from its US and international factories. The Ford factory in Dearborn, Michigan, which is now basically part of Detroit, was at its zenith the largest car factory in the world. It literally had everything in house, even its own electricity.

Ford wrote multiple books, settled in a mansion named Fair Lane not too far away from his factory (Frank Lloyd Wright helped with some of the original designs), and traveled extensively with the likes of Thomas Edison, John Burroughs, Harvey Firestone, and others.

If I had been able to ask Henry Ford a few questions, I think it would have been these:

1. How did you stay sane while organizing the greatest system of self-sufficiency in the world?
2. The Model T came and went. What do you see the future holding?
3. It appears at times that you were slow to change, and that might have hurt the company. Looking back, how would you have advised yourself so you could have done things differently?
4. You made one massive factory be totally self-sufficient. If a country could do the same, would it need to be private-sector or government-driven?

At age 83, Ford died quietly at his Fair Lane home. It was 1947. Clara would follow him three years later, and both would be buried in the Ford Cemetery in Detroit, Michigan.

On the day of his funeral, the city shut down as more than 100,000 people came to pay their last respects to the genius of automobile production. There would never be another like him, but his technology and systems would be used throughout the world.

They say copying is a form of flattery, but it is also one of the surest ways of knowing that you made an impact . . . and copy Henry Ford they did!

Henry Ford **W. Edwards Deming**
1863–1947   1900–1993

Both Henry Ford and W. Edwards Deming were involved in WWII war efforts, but their common bond was working at the Ford company in Dearborn, Michigan. Ford created the Ford Motor Company in 1903, and around 1980, Deming helped save it. Both are in the Automotive Hall of Fame.

CHAPTER 19

W. Edwards Deming

1900-1993

In all the travels and dangers of the Lewis and Clark Expedition (1804–1806), only one member of the team died, and that was from a burst appendix. They were only three months into their almost two-and-a-half-year journey, traveling slowly up the Missouri River, when Charles Floyd quickly got sick and died. He was buried in today's Sioux City, Iowa, on high ground overlooking the river.

If you were to drive by car from Sioux City back down along the Missouri River to St. Louis where the expedition started, it would only take about eight hours. Interesting perspective to say the least.

Almost 100 years later, in 1900, the city of Sioux City created an obelisk to honor Charles Floyd and to mark his grave site. His obelisk looks like a small Washington Monument. It stands 100 feet tall, as compared to the Washington Monument at 555 feet, which had just been completed 15 years earlier.

That same year, W. Edwards Deming was born in Sioux City. The Deming family could trace its origins back to the early Puritans soon after the 1620 *Mayflower* trip.

It seems the Demings were slowly moving west. The transcontinental railroad that connected the US from coast to coast was completed in 1869. It ran through Omaha, Nebraska, which was just 100 miles south along the Missouri River. A lot of the farming and cities were naturally along rivers and train tracks, and then farther and farther out.

When Deming was still a young boy, his family moved even farther west, first to Cody and eventually ending up in the small northwestern Wyoming town of Powell. There they survived rather than thrived in the harsh, rural climate and economy. Both parents would be buried there.

At age 17, Deming traveled to the other end of Wyoming to attend the University of Wyoming. He paid his own way through school, earning an engineering degree. While there, his mother died.

Always a teacher and a lifelong learner, Deming taught physics at the Colorado School of Mines while working on his master's degree in mathematics and physics at the University of Colorado. During this time, he married Agnes Belle, and they soon after adopted a girl who was just over a year old.

During the summers of 1925 and 1926, he worked at the Hawthorne Plant of the Western Electric Company in Chicago. Deming's grandson said that what his grandfather learned those summers made "an impression on him for the rest of his life." Then he attended Yale University where he taught while working on his PhD. Who's to say, but perhaps a few of his Yale predecessors rubbed off on him, such as Noah Webster, Eli Whitney, and Samuel Morse. All those great thinkers were dead and gone, but their influence, creations, and knowledge live on.

> 66 Two basic rules of life are: 1) Change is inevitable.
> 2) Everybody resists change. 99
>
> – W. Edwards Deming

After graduating, Deming took a job at the USDA (United States Department of Agriculture) in Washington, D.C. This was the same time that Henry Ford's Model T was being updated to the Model A, after selling more than 16,000,000 cars worldwide.

Within a few years, Deming would again be giving lectures and writing countless papers. It was his natural passion to teach and to write.

Sadly, his wife died of tuberculosis soon after. That same year, his father also died. I can't imagine how hard that must have been, to lose his parents, as well as his wife. But Deming and his young daughter carried on.

He continued to write and speak. In 1932, he married Lola Shupe, and two years later, their second daughter was born. Life was on the upswing!

All the while, Deming was researching, studying, testing, teaching, and networking. His work for the US government using his skill in statistics and statistical methods opened up opportunity to work with the US Census Bureau. He lowered costs, improved results, and streamlined many aspects of the system.

Admittedly, this may not sound all that exciting or sexy, but what he did was vitally important, and he was about to find out just how important it could be.

Rebuilding After WWII

During the war, Deming was a consultant and advisor while also teaching applied statistics to key people in companies that were helping in the war. If he could make companies better, they could help win the war more quickly.

In 1943, Deming and Lola welcomed their third daughter. That was the same year that George Washington Carver and Edsel Ford died.

After Germany and Japan surrendered in 1945 and WWII came to an end, countries around the world needed help. Deming stepped into the private sector. He wanted to use his skills on a more practical level.

Even though statistics may be taught behind the scenes, its results are very much seen by the public. One example is public elections. In Greece and India, soon after the war while things were still in disarray, he worked as a consultant to observe and apply statistics to their election process.

At the same time, General Douglas MacArthur was in Japan. He had been given the impossible task of helping rebuild Japan, hold war criminals to account, keep the emperor in place, make sure Japan could not start another war, open the country to American business practices, and create a new constitution, among countless other tasks.

MacArthur wisely brought the best of the best to help in that process. In 1947, the same year that Henry Ford died, Deming made his first trip to Japan. He took the friendly stance of being a teacher who wanted students to pass rather than wishing them to fail. He was kind, and after the brutality of war, it was very much appreciated.

Eventually, Deming was given a chance to speak to engineers and managers from across the nation. Using his vast experience with statistical analysis, economies, and growth, he outlined a plan that focused on quality at its core. When everything is built on the continual pursuit of better and better quality, with leadership, training, a good work environment, and self-motivation added on top, success is inevitable.

Countless companies across Japan began to implement Deming's approach and principles. They knew quality exports was the answer for their country, with its limited size and high population, and Deming's principles ideally suited. It wasn't long before they began to see positive results.

The more he spoke and taught, the greater their results from focusing on quality at every level of a company. That meant more profits, lower expenses, bigger markets, happier workers, and eventually global dominance.

No company in its right mind says, "No, thank you" to that list of wins!

> 66 There is not a day I don't think about what Dr. Deming meant to us. Deming is the core of our management. 99
>
> – SHOICHIRO TOYODA, HONORARY CHAIRMAN AND DIRECTOR OF TOYOTA, 1980

Within a few years, the country was already feeling the positive impact. Deming, the teacher of a seemingly very boring subject of statistics, was causing economic waves that were reaching the farthest corners of the globe.

Speaking of cars, if you were to randomly list car companies that are known for continuously producing quality cars, I would be surprised if Toyota is not mentioned as one of the first. They have been pumping out quality products for decades. There's a reason why you don't see very many Toyotas broken down beside the road. And the best-selling car of all time? Yes, it's a Toyota.

Impressed with the returns, Japanese companies offered Deming a royalty as a way of showing their appreciation. Instead, he recommended that they put that money into a prize each year for the company that excels at quality, and that is what they did. Today, the Deming Prize is still a much-coveted award.

In addition to Japan, Deming also brought his applied statistics training to numerous countries outside the United States. At home, he remained virtually unknown.

In 1975, he pretty much retired. He was 75 years old. He had added incredible value to many companies and impacted countless lives.

Finally Reaching US Companies

Around the time he retired, other nations began asking for help—from Japan! You see, Deming had tried to train American companies, but they weren't interested. But when Japanese companies began to outperform American companies, year after year, it was decided that maybe Deming did have something to say after all.

What's funny is that it took a documentary in 1980 called, *If Japan Can, Why Can't We?* aired on American TV to finally get the attention of American companies.

Deming was 80 years old at this point, but suddenly the long-awaited opportunity had come, and he took it at a run!

The Ford car company was one of the first US companies to hire Deming. His business principles helped the Ford company move through some financial challenges, and with fresh focus on quality and listening to customers, they promptly increased their market share. The Ford Taurus success was a direct result of Deming's work with Ford.

Henry Ford would have been proud to see the results, especially the improved efficiency, decreased costs, and improved productivity, not to mention outselling many of his competitors!

> 66 It is not enough to do your best; you must know what to do, and then do your best. 99
>
> – W. EDWARDS DEMING

Every spare moment for Deming was spent speaking, writing books, traveling, training management departments, and basically relaunching himself to a very hungry American audience. Lola often helped edit and crunch numbers for his papers and speeches.

I'm sure the off-the-charts demand for Deming was encouraging and affirming for his family, especially Lola, who had seen Deming work so hard in Japan and elsewhere. They were finally seeing him get the attention he deserved from American companies.

It might have been a little bothersome, too, for US companies had ignored him at their own peril for decades, and now they demanded his help when he should be retired and hanging out with his grandchildren.

But it energized Deming, because in his 80s, he threw away his "I'm retired" sign and planted his "I'm hired" sign instead. Not many people would have been willing, much less had it in them, to be so busy at that age.

Sadly, during those wild relaunching years in the 1980s, both Lola and their first daughter died. Lola was 80 years old, and they had been married for 54 years.

Awards, recognition, and medals continued to come in from multiple countries. Deming had not only received Japan's highest honor that foreigners can receive, the Second Order Medal of the Sacred Treasure, but he was also inducted into the Automotive Hall of Fame. It's the Who's Who of the car world, from owners to racers to inventors, where Henry Ford and Edsel Ford have long been members.

66 Improve quality, you automatically improve productivity. 99

– W. EDWARDS DEMING

At age 93, knowing he was running on borrowed time, Deming created the W. Edwards Deming Institute in the little town of Ketchum, Idaho, to continue his work after he was gone. Incidentally, Ketchum is even farther west than Powell, Wyoming, where he had moved with his parents when he was a little boy.

If I could have sat beside him on the airplane as he was heading to one of his countless trainings across the US, I would have wanted to know:

1. You say you have much to do and little time to do it in. How many years more do you need to do all that you want to do?

2. You seemed to be very patient while you waited for US companies to ask you for help. Were you really patient or were you just busy on other things?

3. Is it possible to achieve full quality control? And if so, what's a normal time frame for this process?

66 A goal without a method is nonsense. 99

– W. EDWARDS DEMING

Later that year (1993), just days after giving a speech, Deming died from cancer at his home in Washington, D.C. His and Lola's urns are today side by side in the Saint Columba's Episcopal Church Columbarium in Washington, D.C.

Today, the work continues at the W. Edwards Deming Institute.

Who knew that statistics could be so exciting and so practical! But the proof is always in the fruit, and looking at Deming's results, and the continued results in countless companies around the world today, you know it worked!

That is a legacy we should all hope to leave.

CONCLUSION

Knowing the roots of our country, for better or for worse, gives us a healthy appreciation of the journey we made and how lucky we are to live here in this day, in this land. Armed with the knowledge of history, we can make decisions that could have generational impact for the better.

I love my country wholeheartedly and believe that history, as it happened, not as we choose to remember it, is the best recipe for success. Never sacrifice what you know for what is cool or "in" at the time because history does not respond to public opinion. The truth will endure.

ACKNOWLEDGMENTS

My wife, Kate, for always putting up with me.

My parents, for imparting to me how important it is to learn from history.

Chris Ruddy, for taking a chance on an unknown.

The heroes in our lives, who help shape our futures.

ABOUT THE AUTHOR

Carl Higbie is a former Navy SEAL, Senior Appointee to President Trump, and currently the host of Newsmax's *Carl Higbie Frontline*. Carl Higbie was born in 1983 in southwestern Connecticut. He was a state champion wrestler in high school, and attended Sacred Heart University until the war on terror was declared. In 2003, Carl dropped out of college, leaving behind a promising wrestling career, and enlisted to become a US Navy SEAL. He completed two combat deployments to Iraq in 2007 and 2009 where he and his team captured the infamous "Butcher of Fallujah."

Subsequently, he returned to take a senior training position for his remaining three years where he taught high-risk evolutions such as Close Quarters Combat and Air Operations. It was during this time that Carl released his first book *Battle on the Home Front*, which brought to light many problems, some political in nature, that were plaguing our country and the military. The book led to a highly publicized battle against a politically charged machine reaching to the White House. Two years after leaving the military, Carl emerged victorious against all odds, which his new book *Enemies Foreign and Domestic* is based on.

With a victory against political correctness under his belt, at 30 years old, he took on a run for US Congress in 2014, losing a contentious convention in a five-way race garnering 14 percent on his first run—more than any other candidate outside of the party favorite who received over three quarters of the total 265 votes. He then published his third book, *Crises of Culture: The Political Battlefield of the New Civil War.*

Carl Higbie has owned three successful businesses in his tenure, including his current consulting firm Ameriman LLC. He has been an integral player on dozens of campaigns including President Trump's chief surrogate during the campaign, as well as the communication director and Spokesman for Great America Super PAC.

He currently sits on the advisory board of Pipe Hitter Foundation. He served as a presidential appointee as the Chief of External Affairs for the Corporation for National and Community Service, was the Director of Advocacy for America First Policy and America First Action, and a senior policy advisor for the Urban Revitalization Coalition, an executive order authorized nationwide project. Higbie is one of the most respected authorities on politics, the military, and national security. His natural leadership skills coupled with his experience as a Navy SEAL make Higbie uniquely qualified to comment on a range of issues.

Visit Carl Higbie: CarlHigbie.com

For more information, visit
Newsmaxtv.com/Shows/Carl-Higbie-Frontline